Insurrection & Revolution

Studies in Cuban History
Series Editor: Louis A. Pérez Jr.

Politics of Illusion: The Bay of Pigs Invasion Reexamined,
edited by James G. Blight and Peter Kornbluh

Insurrection and Revolution: Armed Struggle in Cuba, 1952–1959,
Gladys Marel García-Pérez

Prologue to Revolution: Cuba, 1898–1958,
Jorge Ibarra

INSURRECTION & REVOLUTION

Armed Struggle in Cuba, 1952–1959

Gladys Marel García-Pérez

translated by Juan Ortega

LYNNE
RIENNER
PUBLISHERS

BOULDER
LONDON

Published in the United States of America in 1998 by
Lynne Rienner Publishers, Inc.
1800 30th Street, Boulder, Colorado 80301

and in the United Kingdom by
Lynne Rienner Publishers, Inc.
3 Henrietta Street, Covent Garden, London WC2E 8LU

Library of Congress Cataloging-in-Publication Data
García-Pérez, Gladys Marel.
  Insurrection and revolution : armed struggle in Cuba, 1952–1959 /
  Gladys Marel García-Pérez : translated by Juan Ortega.
    p.   cm.—(Studies in Cuban history)
  Includes bibliographical references and index.
  ISBN 1-55587-611-0 (alk. paper)
    1. Cuba—History—1933–1959. 2. Matanzas (Cuba : Province)—
History. 3. Movimiento Revolucionario 26 de Julio. 4. Government,
Resistance to—Cuba—Matanzas (Province)—History. 5. Cuba—
Economic policy. I. Title. II. Series.
F1787.5.G37   1998
972.9106'3—dc21   97-49997
                                                              CIP

British Cataloguing in Publication Data
A Cataloguing in Publication record for this book
is available from the British Library.

Printed and bound in the United States of America

  The paper used in this publication meets the requirements
∞ of the American National Standard for Permanence of
  Paper for Printed Library Materials Z39.48-1984.

5 4 3 2 1

Al otro Fidel

Contents

Foreword, Louis A. Pérez Jr.   ix
Preface   xi
Map of Cuba   xiv

1   The Military Coup and Its Aftermath   1

2   A Generation on the March   13

3   The Political Economy of the Batista Government   33

4   The July 26 Movement:
    Spontaneous Mobilization, Resistance, and Insurrection   61

5   Armed Struggle, Workers, and Guerrilla War   81

6   Toward January 1, 1959   99

List of Acronyms   109

Chronology   111

Notes   115

Index   127
About the Book   138

Foreword

Louis A. Pérez Jr.

A vast literature has formed around the Cuban revolution, in all its multiple facets and its many phases. Much of the scholarship outside of Cuba has tended to concentrate on the years after 1959, following the triumph of the revolutionary war, during which Cuba underwent successive waves of transformation. Research interest in the period between 1952 and 1959, however, spanning the military coup of Fulgencio Batista and the deepening opposition to the Batista regime, has receded. The early renderings of these years thus persist as the dominant versions of the insurrectionary struggle, derived principally from images of the triumphant rebel army under Fidel Castro in the Sierra Maestra and of guerrilla columns under the command of Raúl Castro, Juan Almeida, Camilo Cienfuegos, and Ernesto (Ché) Guevara. In some of the more nuanced accounts, attention is perhaps expanded to include the civic resistance, the Revolutionary Directorate (Directorio Revolucionario; DR), and the II Front Escambray.

In contrast, this book explores the regional bases of support for the July 26 Revolutionary Movement (Movimiento Revolucionario 26 Julio; MR 26-7) in Matanzas Province, far removed from the Sierra Maestra. Drawing on archival research, extensive oral histories, and a careful review of the provincial press, Gladys Marel García-Pérez examines the nature of local support for armed struggle against the Batista government. She argues that the MR 26-7 functioned effectively at a grassroots level precisely because it incorporated into the widely used methods of armed resistance those forms developed locally and often spontaneously in response to local conditions and daily concerns.

The great value of this study lies in its successful redressing of the historiographic imbalance that at present characterizes the

literature dealing with the insurrectionary war. García-Pérez's ex-
amination of the grassroots support extended to MR 26-7 under-
scores the importance of local participation. Attention thus shifts
from the heroic and highly visible guerrilla *comandantes* to the many
men and women who participated, typically in anonymity, in what
must be considered the front lines of the armed struggle against the
Batista government. Indeed, anonymity was essential to the success
of the local resistance—to be identified was often tantamount to a
death sentence. The historiographic implications of anonymity are,
of course, immediately obvious.

García-Pérez rescues from oblivion the men and women who
participated in and around the urban fronts of the insurrectionary
war. What makes her study all the more compelling, and in many
ways possible at all, is that its insights are derived not only from
thorough research but also from the experience of the author, who
was herself a participant in many of the activities she chronicles, a
friend to many of the people she mentions, a witness to many of
the events she describes. García-Pérez is thus in a unique position
to deepen our understanding of one of the important theaters of
the war.

It is to be hoped that this book will also serve to stimulate new
research on the 1952–1959 period. More studies are needed at the
provincial and municipal levels, out of Havana and from the interior. Only through this type of investigation will it be possible to
develop a fuller understanding of the purpose of and participation
in what was one of the most successful popular revolutionary
movements of the twentieth century.

Preface

Between 1952 and 1959, in the course of struggle between the government of Fulgencio Batista and the revolutionary forces, the vital issue of who would hold political power was definitively settled.

The revolutionary movement began immediately after the military coup of 1952 and expanded to include diverse organizations and opposition groups, both those that believed in armed struggle and those that opposed it in favor of other forms of resistance. Building on structures that could accommodate various opposition sectors, the July 26 Revolutionary Movement (MR 26-7) emerged as the key instrument of the success of the insurgent movement. Despite tactical differences among the various insurrectional groups, all shared one unifying objective: overthrow of the regime.

This study examines the evolution, integration, and tactics of the national liberation movement in the province of Matanzas. Two fundamental hypotheses guide the work: Popular rebellion developed within the complex fabric of society by its own methods, and the MR 26-7 appropriated those methods as part of its tactics to overthrow the Batista regime. I seek to assess the development of the popular revolts, their manner of coalescing, and their method of operation against the Batista government. I also review the impact that national events had on the development of insurgency in the provinces.

Cuban historiography has left untouched many of the key issues of this period. Foreign historians likewise have failed to deal with the local, regional, and provincial history of the revolution. There has been a tendency, for example, to portray the protest of the University Student Federation (Federación Estudiantil Universitaria; FEU) at the University of Havana on March 10, 1952, as the only outward expression of collective protest, ignoring actions elsewhere in the country.

In contrast, the study of regional and provincial history allows the researcher to arrive at a fuller understanding of the composition and purpose of a popular movement. For this reason I focus on Matanzas. The role of this province was central to the success of the insurrection, but it is a role that is virtually unknown.

*   *   *

During more than two decades of research related to the Cuban revolution and the study of the generational crisis, I received help from numerous institutions, colleagues, and friends. Their advice on a wide range of matters has been of inestimable value.

I am grateful for the unflagging assistance of specialists, technicians, and administrative staffs at the Archivo Nacional de Cuba, the Instituto de Ciencias Sociales de la Academia de Ciencias de Cuba, the Instituto de Historia de Cuba, the Oficina de Asuntos Históricos del Consejo de Estado, the Biblioteca Nacional "José Martí," the Archivo Provincial de Matanzas, the Museo de la Revolución, la Sección de Historia Provincial de Matanzas, and the Archivos de las Casas de los Combatientes de la Lucha Clandestina and Guerrillera of all fourteen municipalities of Matanzas Province and of the Plaza de la Revolución, Centro Habana, and Madruga in Havana Province and Corralillo in Las Villas Province. I am particularly indebted to Otto Hernández, Pedro Alvarez Tabío, and Haydée Díaz of the Consejo de Estado. Julio Vargas at the Archivo Nacional was an indispensable collaborator. I also owe an enormous debt to Saul Vento, Graciela and her staff at the Archivo Provincial de Matanzas, and Octavio Louis Cabrera in the Archivo de la Casa de Combatientes de Plaza de la Revolución.

A great many persons contributed to the success of the fieldwork related to this research. More than 300 combatants, collaborators, and leaders participated in the oral history phase of the project and generously provided me with access to unpublished documents. Special mention must be made of Oscar Gutiérrez Barceló and Leandro Marín, who played a key role in identifying participants in the insurrection in the region of Cárdenas and who planned meetings with individuals and groups. Emérito García y Corogua helped arrange interviews and meetings in Jagüey Grande, Agramonte, and Unión de Reyes. Francisco (El Chino) Fontela underwrote the costs associated with the interviews and meetings on more than one occasion. Among the many others who assisted in promoting the meetings and facilitating contacts in the vast expanses of the national territory were Pedro Ferreira and Arturo Lantigua in Matanzas, Ceiba Mocha, and Madruga; Aída Manresa and her brothers in Madruga; and Víctor Guerra and Faña and Edilio Díaz Crespo (Tin). Rafael (Chichi) Trujillo set up the interview with the group from Bolondrón.

Similarly, Héctor Rodríguez, who understood from the outset the objectives of the study, provided important support from the National Bank. Elena Alavez, with her experience as head of the "Sección de Historia" of *Bohemia* magazine, and Vivián Abreu provided me with wise counsel and critical assistance in the last phases of writing the book, as did Isabel Zamora and the provincial leaders Ricardo González Trejo and Felipe Quintana. They have my sincerest gratitude.

I also wish to mention the valuable assistance of historian Clara Emilia Chávez in making meetings in Matanzas possible and providing research teams to aid in my work. And a special thanks to Esteban Lazo, without whom I would have been unable to complete my study of nearly 1,000 files of the fourteen municipalities or organize the final group meetings in Cárdenas and Colón. The historian Verónica Rodríguez, member of the research team from the Academy of Sciences, aided in the completion of the oral history project and the collection of archival materials.

I thank my friend and colleague Jorge Ibarra for the rigor of his responses to the manuscript during the final stages of its preparation. Jorge was a source of support for my work during a critical time, and I owe him a great debt of gratitude. Special thanks as well to Teresita Iglesias and John Dumolin.

I owe a debt of gratitude, too, to my friend and colleague Louis A. Pérez Jr., whose opinions and suggestions have been invaluable to me. I must also acknowledge friends who aided my work at the University of South Florida and the University of North Carolina–Chapel Hill. And thank you to my son Michel Suzarte for his computer expertise and to Juan Ortega for his translation.

I cannot omit a special thanks for everything to the person to whom this book is dedicated, *el otro Fidel,* my husband, without whom I would not have been able to complete this book or—why not simply admit it?—to survive. His material help, his technical assistance, and his personal talents guaranteed that the oral history project was successfully completed.

A mi pueblo. Por inspirarme el amor tan profundo que le profeso. Por ello, dedico mi vida a escribir su historia.

G. M. G.-P.
Havana

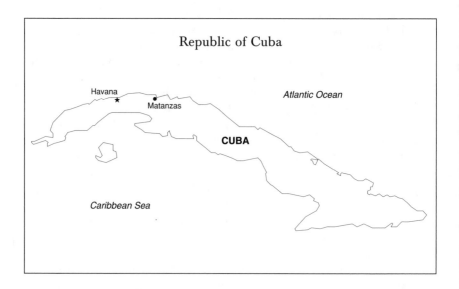

Republic of Cuba

Havana

Matanzas

Atlantic Ocean

CUBA

Caribbean Sea

1

The Military Coup and Its Aftermath

Nearly eight years after having retired as president of Cuba and after several years of residency in the United States, Fulgencio Batista y Zaldívar returned to Cuba in 1951, under the protection of the political immunity granted by the Auténtico government of Carlos Prío Socarrás, authorized to run again for the presidency of the republic. At the same time, in 1951–1952, a conspiracy was developing within the Cuban armed forces. Perhaps the most salient of its diverse motives involved a nationalist impulse. Batista, with characteristic shrewdness, established contact with these nationalist elements, although the movement itself was of no intrinsic interest to him. And with the death in 1951 of Eduardo Chibás, leader of the Ortodoxo Party, he considered the road to power once again clear.

On March 10, 1952, Batista succeeded in placing himself at the head of a military coup that promised to provide stability and order to the republic. As in the coup of September 4, 1933, when he led an enlisted men's sedition against officer corps and eventually against the government of Carlos Manuel de Céspedes (an action known as the "Sergeants' Revolt"), Batista used sedition within the armed forces to facilitate his ascendancy to political power.

The diverse and conflicting factions within the armed forces led to the weakening and eventual collapse of the military. But blinded by personal ambitions, Batista failed to see what was happening. He established a regime of force based on the promulgation of new statutes and decrees and abolished the 1940 constitution. He revived the banner of September 4, 1933, as a symbol, affirming his commitment to containing the forces of social disorder and political instability. He insisted that the basis of his government in 1952 rested on the unity of the armed forces, though in fact this was more apparent than real.

Certainly Batista used the armed forces as an instrument of force to maintain himself in power and combat any opposition. But there existed within the military a frustrated nationalist-revolutionary tendency that he sought to eliminate but that expanded between 1952 and 1959. Nevertheless, he appointed to high positions within the army command a coterie of Septembrista officers who were personally and politically loyal to him, headed by General Francisco Tabernilla Dolz and members of his family. The group also included General Eulogio Cantillo Porras and his brother Carlos.

The rebellion Batista organized in Havana first reverberated in the army during the early hours of March 10, 1952, among the regiments of Las Villas, Camagüey, and Oriente. These regiments initially remained loyal to the government and the 1940 constitution. Colonel Eduardo Martín Elena and Colonel Manuel Alvarez Margolles, commander of the Oriente regiment, denounced the coup as illegal and unconstitutional, and they informed President Carlos Prío that they were prepared to resist it with force.

As Colonel Martín Elena held the Matanzas military garrison loyal to the Auténtico government, crowds converged on the park and the regimental headquarters asking for weapons to combat Batista's coup d'état. Among those who rallied to defend the beleaguered government were students, professionals, workers, and members of the Ortodoxo and the Auténtico Parties. They often reacted spontaneously without political leadership to guide their actions, their improvised demonstrations, strikes, and sabotage—precisely the elements that would characterize the tactics of Cuban insurgency during 1952–1959.

People in Las Villas, Matanzas, Havana, and Oriente took to the streets and parks to protest the coup, and students and workers called for a general strike.[1] The most prominent role was assumed by the FEU, which was catapulted to the head of the civic-patriotic resistance movement in the aftermath of the coup.

Despite the significant popular support the Ortodoxos and (to a somewhat lesser degree) the Auténticos enjoyed in the municipalities of Matanzas, Batista was nevertheless able to seize power. Batista's success was due in part to his experience during the 1933–1934 seditions, which allowed him to establish a certain continuity to Septembrismo—the politics of the army officers who rose to power after the September 1933 coup—and unite different groups around the military. He had demonstrated his skills by ousting the 1933 provisional government and manipulating the many and conflicting interests of the political parties. He was also successful in dealing with the controversial issues of administrative corruption and gangsterism. Batista had further proved himself in his handling of matters of interest to the United States in Cuba. He had, for example, contained the nationalist-revolutionary and leftist tendencies that raised the specter of a populist government, such as that of Jacobo Arbenz in Guatemala, which would have challenged foreign economic interests in Cuba.

Batista was able to thwart the Ortodoxo Party in the 1952 election, thereby keeping power from a party associated with patriotism, domestic restructuring, honest administration, and public integrity. The party of Eduardo Chibás would have set up a united government in which the interests of the middle classes would have prevailed, contributing to the emergence of a liberal bourgeois democracy with a program of popular reforms.[2]

The campaign against administration corruption was launched during the Auténtico government (1948–1952) with the actions of three officials of Ortodoxo origins appointed by President Carlos Prío to head the National Bank, the Agriculture Bank, and the Tobacco Stabilization Fund: Felipe Pazos, Justo Carrillo, and José Miguel Irisarri, all former members of the Directorate of University Students (Directorio Estudiantil Universitario; DEU) who opposed the regime of force set up on March 10, 1952, and resigned from their posts on the very same day.[3]

Ortodoxo professors such as Rafael García Bárcenas, Herminio Portell Vilá, Roberto Agramonte, and Salvador Massip taught the young officers attending the military academy respect for civilian rule and military professionalism. They instilled in these officers unconnected to the Septembrista generation a sense of integrity, gaining followers and sympathizers for Ortodoxo policies who rejected the Auténtico and Batista regimes. This group became known as the *puros*.

The concept of *puro* was rooted in the purity associated with the patriotic ideals of a well-ordered republic without political privileges—that is, the *puros* opposed twentieth-century politicking, the deals and rake-offs that characterized the decades following the frustrated 1930 revolution. This generation of republicans included young workers, students, and professionals, some committed to individual political parties, others without political affiliation.

In Matanzas student and worker demonstrations were indicative of the continuity of the province's patriotic traditions. Every year many of these groups marched to El Morrillo, the site of Antonio

Guiteras's murder by Batista's army in an ambush in Matanzas in 1935. A member of the 1933 revolutionary government and founder and leader of the organization Young Cuba (Joven Cuba), Guiteras had confronted Batista prior to the first January 1934 coup. The murder of the progressive leader effectively crushed the popular insurrection against Batista in the 1930s but created a martyr who served as a symbol of resistance and rebellion in the later struggle against Batista.

* * *

In 1949 the corruption and vice led to a crisis in the Cuban political and military organization that deepened through late 1951 and early 1952. The crisis in the military sector was reflected mainly within three groups: The first were the junior officers and cadets known as the *puros*. The second group, made up principally of captains and lieutenants, included the so-called *tanquistas* (tankists), the corrupt, hard-line commanders who played key roles in the March coup. The final group consisted of retired officers, both Batista's Septembristas and Auténticos who feared being displaced by a new government.

Restless and disappointed with the civilian government, the *puros* decided to overthrow the Auténtico regime. They planned to set up a military junta, reestablish order, and convene national elections to create a new government that would include among its policies political and administrative reforms.[4]

At the outset the conspirators considered appointing Major Ramón Barquín, the director of the military academy, to preside over the junta, but they later decided that Batista was more capable of controlling public opinion.[5] In February 1952 they asked Batista to take a stand and seize power.[6]

During the first week of March, the conspirators held their final meetings in the home of former captain Fernández Miranda. Among the officers who attended were Lieutenant Rafael Salas Cañizares; Captain Dámaso Sogo; Lieutenant Pedro Barrera Pérez; former general Francisco Tabernilla Dolz (loyal to and personal friend of Batista since 1933); Captains Luis Robaina Piedra, Jorge García Tuñón, and Juan Rojas González; and Lieutenants Artemio Pérez Díaz, Ignacio Leonard Castell, and Armando Echemendía Leyva. They made detailed plans and assigned all military positions by the second week in March.[7]

Batista attended the March 9 political rally in Matanzas to deflect any suspicion regarding the impending coup. The rebels, civilians and military alike, met at midnight on Batista's estate, from which they went on to the Columbia military headquarters in Havana. Batista and ten officers led the move on Columbia. The officer in charge, Captain Dámaso Sogo, opened the way for Batista. As some officers took command of the four infantry battalions and mobilized the garrison's troops, a group of young officers imprisoned the chiefs of the army in their residences located on the military base.

Some fifty conspirators went to control points while Lieutenant Pedro Rodríguez Avila of the tank battalion blocked off all access points to Columbia with armored vehicles. That morning 1,000 officers were arrested by armored detachments. Most of them were immediately removed from the armed forces for failing to join the insurrection.[8]

As planned, General Francisco Tabernilla took command of La Cabaña fortress. Captain José Rodríguez Calderón took over the navy, including the Castillo de la Punta fortress; he was immediately promoted, as were the naval officers who had participated and supported the conspiracy. Salas Cañizares occupied police headquarters and the main offices of the telephone company, from where he controlled all lines to the presidential palace. As of that moment, the conspirators were able to monitor communications between President Prío and provincial regimental commands, including the Matanzas Plácido Regiment.[9]

Carlos Prío departed Havana for the city of Matanzas at 8:30 A.M. Tanks from Columbia under the command of Captain José Miguel Alvarez de la Noval and Lieutenant Raúl Corzo Izaguirre immediately seized the presidential palace. Machine guns were set up on the roofs surrounding the palace. An exchange of gunfire had already taken place early in the morning; police lieutenant Julián Negret died, and two government officers were wounded.

Batista organized the military groups as he had done for the coup of September 4, 1933. The sole difference was that instead of organizing sergeants and enlisted men, on this occasion he organized captains and lieutenants who, under the command of the Septembristas, took over the vital structures of the army, police, navy, and main government offices.

During the morning of March 10, control of all provincial regiments passed into the hands of the conspirators. A rebellion of officers forced Colonel Martín Elena of Matanzas to relinquish command. When asked to join the conspirators, he said, "You wear the stars of the colonel, but I shall not stain my career by supporting a coup against the republic. I shall never violate the constitution." He was arrested in the regiment's club, where the September 4 banner was raised.[10]

Shortly afterward President Prío arrived at his last stronghold, the capital of Matanzas, where the overthrow of the Auténtico government was consummated. He went to the residence of Mayor Pedro Uría and called the Mexican embassy to request political asylum. A few weeks later, he left for Miami with Aureliano Sánchez Arango, Eugenio Soler, and other supporters.

* * *

Several sectors of Cuban society headed a growing spontaneous rebellion against the coup d'état in March 1952.[11] The public and the press recalled the March 1935 events that had led to a general strike and the repression launched by Batista's regime. In editorials, manifestos, and other publications, the FEU and the media described this collective memory as well as the new role of the students as standard-bearers in the defense of the constitution and democracy.

Workers and students sought to organize a strike. They could not keep the regime from consolidating its power but employed a method of popular struggle that would later be part of the tactics of the insurgent youth: They formed a generational vanguard of elements from several sectors of society organized into a political, civic, and military structure.

While the conspirators took over government offices, worker and professional groups started arriving at the University of Havana to join the students' rebellion. The Cuban flag waved at half mast on campus. The FEU held a plenary session and agreed to "begin an indefinite strike and actively support and defend civilian power." Trade union leaders Facundo Pomar of the Omnibus Aliados and Marcos Hirigoyen of the Autobuses Modernos exchanged ideas with the students.[12]

The Student Federation of the Institute of Matanzas (Federación Estudiantil del Instituto de Matanzas; FEIM), worker federations, and different trade unions of the province of Matanzas organized the strike. Both the student and worker sectors were linked to political parties and expected weapons that Colonel Martín Elena was supposedly going to distribute before the arms fell into the hands of the conspirators. Similar events took place in the cities of Cárdenas, Colón, Jovellanos, and Agramonte. With the same spontaneity, people went to high schools, parks, city halls, and garrisons. The FEU published its "Declaration of Principles" on March 14 and during the following months continued to accuse Batista of having stained the honor of the *patria* (fatherland).

The Provincial Federation of Textile Workers (Federación Provincial de Trabajadores Textileras; FPTT) in Matanzas maintained a noteworthy position. Ortodoxo leader Julián Alemán, secretary-general of the federation, organized the general strike that had been called for from Havana by the Auténtico union leader Pascasio Lineras, head of the National Federal of Textile Workers (Federación Nacional de Trabajadores Textiles; FNTT) and member of the Confederation of Cuban Workers (Confederación de Trabajadores Cubanos; CTC).

In the western part of the country, textile and hemp industry union leaders carried out strikes over several months, demanding unpaid wages. The plantations located in Camarioca, Cárdenas, and Carboneras were in the foreground of this social struggle.

The trade union of the Matanzas rayon mill began the strike movement that expanded to Havana's Textilera Arigüanabo, Guanajay's Cuban Cordage, and Matanzas Jarcía. The textile and rayon workers stood out in the strike movement as a result of their strong Ortodoxo trade union leadership and the active participation of all union members. Groups of linemen from the Cuban Electric Power Company also distinguished themselves in antigovernment activities after March 10. The mills in Calabazar in Havana shut down, and the strike reached all of Havana's major department stores, bringing about a total work stoppage. Consequently, the government disbanded the Instituto del Henequén, a source of antigovernment plots. The textile workers' federation confirmed that some 30,000 workers had joined the strike. Arrests were massive. As the strikes increased, the regime appointed military supervisors to handle negotiations with local trade unions and settle worker-employer conflicts.

* * *

Batista created a hard-line government in 1952 in much the same manner he had done in 1934. He set up the military junta in Camp Columbia and appointed a government under his leadership as prime minister. His ministers were Miguel Angel de la Campa (State), Miguel Angel Céspedes (Justice), Ramón O. Hermida (Interior), Marino López Blanco (Treasury), José A. Mandigutía (Public Works), Alfredo Jacomino (Agriculture), Oscar de la Torre

(Trade), Jesús A. Portocarrero (Labor), Andrés Rivero Agüero (Education), Enrique Saladrigas Zayas (Health and Public Welfare), Pablo Carrera Justiz (Communications), and Nicolás Pérez Hernández (National Defense).

Batista also abolished the presidency and vice presidency, suspended congress, and replaced the legislative body with a consultative council composed of eighty members, led by Carlos Saladrigas and Oscar García Montes.

U.S. ambassador William Beaulac visited the new minister of foreign affairs, Miguel de la Campa, on March 27 to inform him that the United States had recognized his government, whose policies were in line with U.S. interests.[13] Long before the coup d'état, the U.S. media suspected its coming. U.S. journalist Francis McCarthy had held a private interview with Batista in 1951 on this question. Elliot Roosevelt, visiting Havana in 1952 with a delegation of shipowners interested in setting up several businesses, talked with Batista on behalf of a TV station. Once the coup had been consummated, U.S. Steel Company officials visited the regime's minister of information, Ernesto de la Fe, to stress that U.S. capital was responding favorably and assure the government that the United States would supply Cuba with everything it needed.[14]

With the recognition of Batista's regime by the governments of the United States, Latin America, and Europe, international political propaganda projected the image of a Batista consolidated in power and backed by armed forces. In fact, that unity was nonexistent. Military conspiracies against the Batista government persisted, in large measure directed against the Septembristas and the *tanquistas*. Batista failed to fulfill the civic-military aims of the *puros* and instead gave command to the most inefficient personnel, granting promotions to those officers and soldiers who had participated in and supported the coup.

The disgust of many young officers was momentarily quelled when air force chief Colonel Cantillo, of unquestionable professional prestige, joined the coup. Dissatisfaction returned, however, and the directors of the officers' school attempted to dispel it by reducing the curriculum by one year, thus weakening the relationship between promotions and academic advance.

After the coup, opposition groups in Havana organized underground activities that involved both military and civilians from a cross-section of social sectors. In March 1952 Rafael García Bárcenas, who had participated in the government of 1933, organized a civilian and military coalition at the University of Havana known as the National Revolutionary Movement (Movimiento Nacionalista Revolucionario; MNR). It was composed of young workers, professionals, and others who belonged to the university student movement and the youth of the Ortodoxo and Auténtico Parties. Bárcenas and more than twenty of his followers were imprisoned when they attacked Camp Columbia in April 1953. Most of the leaders and civilian members of the MNR later joined the July 26 Revolutionary Movement (Movimiento Revolucionario 26 Julio; MR 26-7) led by Fidel Castro.

Another group that joined the *puro* officers in Havana was led by Ramón Barquín and Major Enrique Borbonet. Barquín, who had previously lived in the United States, visited Borbonet during a trip to Havana and agreed to develop a consensus within the military cadre for the purpose of organizing a rebellion.

The conspirators met in April 1956 at Barquín's residence in the military district of Tarará beach in Havana. According to their plans, the sedition would take place in Havana. Borbonet was to assume command of Camp Columbia, Colonel Manuel Varela Castro was to seize the tank regiment, and Barquín planned to move against the chiefs of staff. Manuel Villafaña would assume command of the air force headquarters, Major José Orihuela Torras was to take the La Cabaña headquarters, and Lieutenant José Fernández Alvarez was to seize the Managua military base. These officers would then communicate with the former chief of Matanzas regiment, Colonel Martín Elena, who would take charge of police headquarters. Colonel Driggs was to control the navy, and Major Clemente Gómez Sicre would seize Military Intelligence Service (Servicio de Inteligencia Militar; SIM) headquarters. Borbonet would send a detachment to occupy the Kuquine farm, Batista's estate. Major Tomás Cabañas was to assume command of the Matanzas regiment; Major Elías Monteagudo Fleites, Regiment Five; and Captain Enrique Cué Somarriba, Pinar del Río's Regiment Eight. Cabañas was always to remain chief of the Matanzas military forces.

Barquín coordinated his civilian-related actions with Justo Carrillo, a prominent student leader of the 1930s and later a member of the Ortodoxo Party, and his Liberation Action (Acción Libertadora) organization (later known as the Montecristi Group). Carrillo would be responsible for appointing the new cabinet.

The April 4 conspiracy was discovered a few weeks after Ortodoxo senator Pelayo Cuervo publicly denounced the existence of a group of Trujillistas (admirers of Dominican Republican president Rafael Trujillo) within the March 10 forces. A plot was indeed under way, but the group was actually made up of putschist March 10 officers, unhappy with the Tabernilla family's control over appointments to key commands.

The conspiracy shook the country to its roots, as part of the army rebelled against another sector of the army.[15]

* * *

The year 1955 was a milestone in the disintegration of Batista's regime. Discontent within the armed forces intensified. In mid-1955, during a tour of U.S. military facilities, General Díaz Tamayo attributed this unrest to Batista's accumulation of wealth.

The military conspiracies of the *puros* and *tanquistas,* followed by a naval uprising in Cienfuegos in 1957 and the refusal of air force pilots to obey orders to bomb the city, revealed the process of disintegration.

There was no evidence of the *puro* conspiracy in the province of Matanzas. But several members of the armed forces did participate in or cooperate with seditious action within the army itself or in the MR 26-7. The most significant of these events was the agreement between a group of officers and policemen of the Martí municipality with the MR 26-7 regional leadership in Cárdenas to attack the police station and seize all weapons shortly before the strike of April 9, 1958. The plan was not carried out until December 1958 by a local guerrilla group of the MR 26-7 under the command of Lázaro Blanco. The Cienfuegos uprising was also backed by the movement's provincial leadership, which sabotaged stores and communications.[16]

Sedition slowly undermined the armed forces from within, culminating in 1958 with widespread desertion of officers and soldiers to the rebel forces. Many, however, considered resignation an act of cowardice and resolved to wait for the right moment to fight against the regime. The Septembrista officers, aware of discontent, used bribery in an attempt to gain support.

One of the most prominent officers in the class of 1951 of the military academy was Guillermo Morales. During Batista's army offensive against MR 26-7 in the eastern provinces several years later, Morales was dispatched to the theater of operations. The danger of guerrilla ambushes was constant, and the government's army command post abandoned its troops without food for two days, ignoring a request for a helicopter to transport the wounded. The senior military command of the regime also refused to back up the troops fighting in Las Mercedes near the Sierra Maestra. Once these soldiers were transferred to Bayamo, they entered into a conspiracy against the regime. After Fidel Castro sent an open letter to officers and troops asking soldiers instead to join the rebel forces, the fifty-man platoon led by Morales crossed over into rebel-held territory.[17]

The army's morale continued to deteriorate. By late 1958 government troops were no longer attacking Matanzas guerrilla groups, who had established their base of operations center between Colón and Cárdenas.[18] The legend surrounding Batista waned throughout 1958, whereas the MR 26-7's reputation was enhanced. A much more powerful myth also vanished: that of being able to fight with the army or without the army, but never against the army assisted and supplied by the government of the United States. The armed forces of the first republic (1902) that emerged from the liberation army ceased to exist at the end of Batista's regime.

The U.S. ambassador to Cuba established a consultative group of U.S. businessmen in Cuba in spring 1958. At a meeting in December 1958, they decided the "Cuban situation was deteriorating very rapidly" and unless the United States provided support, Batista was unlikely to last beyond February 24, 1959, the date his term of office formally expired, and "even with such support, it was doubtful he could hold out" till the end of his term. In a memo to the U.S. sectretary of state, a member of the group advised, "Since it was inconceivable that [the U.S. government] aid Castro, and since [it was] probably too late to help Batista, the U.S. should promote and give full support, including arms, to a military civilian junta. The . . . junta would be more likely to enlist wide popular support and would weaken Castro."[19]

Batista's crisis during the first few months of 1958 reflected the rupture between the government and social, fraternal, and religious institutions and elements of the upper classes—an indication of the regime's imminent collapse that began during the April 1958 strike. In view of this situation, Batista did not consider a dialogue with the opposition political parties but rather with the rebel forces in the Sierra Maestra through the National Harmony Commission established by the Catholic Church. Seeking an agreement with the forces that most threatened him, he demanded weapons from the United States to bolster his strength.

The U.S. government instead mobilized its naval forces for possible evacuation of U.S. citizens living in the eastern provinces.

* * *

The strong popular movement in Matanzas Province was led principally by the FEU, FEIM, and the Ortodoxo, Auténtico, and

Socialist Parties. In the provincial capital as well as in Havana, joint student-worker actions were coordinated by the FEU, FEIM, and the trade unions and on occasion resulted in political demonstrations and labor strikes in cooperation with Ortodoxo workers. Among the most notable events of 1952–1958 were the demonstrations commemorating the assassination of Antonio Guiteras in which student leaders joined with the FPTT of the Matanzas rayon mill. In 1955 a sugar strike in Matanzas organized by the National Federation of Sugar Workers (Federación Nacional de Trabajadores Azucareros; FNTA) was supported by the student leadership.

As part of his strategy to hold power, Batista used violence but also governed by "statutes" that allowed him to suspend constitutional guarantees at will.[20] Batista further pursued an economic strategy designed to develop monopoly and bureaucratic capital in the country, maintaining military control over employer-worker conflicts and reaffirming traditional Cuban-U.S. relations.

The mutual assistance bilateral treaty and the U.S. advisory mission (made up of advisers from the U.S. Army, Navy, and Air Forces) ensured Batista military consultancy services and war supplies almost to the end of his rule. Up to March 1958, President Dwight D. Eisenhower supported the regime through its political-military structures on the island. In return the Cuban government sought to guarantee the lives and property of U.S. citizens in Cuba. As of 1957 these guarantees were seriously endangered and by 1958 became critical with the qualitative change in the balance of forces in favor of the revolutionary movement, particularly in Oriente Province, the site of substantial U.S. investments.

As the insurrection gained momentum during 1957–1958, a government in arms was set up in territories liberated by the MR 26-7 rebel army despite the U.S government's support of the Batista regime. Washington maintained its policy until the regime's overthrow and specifically opposed the insurgent leadership of the MR 26-7 and the Revolutionary Directorate (Directorio Revolucionario; DR) March 13—organizations Batista claimed were communist.

2

A Generation on the March

The insurgency in Cuba (1952–1958), as the first stage of the revolution, had its origins in the immediate aftermath of the military coup led by Fulgencio Batista in March 1952. The democratic-liberal juncture that allowed the Ortodoxo Party to win the June 1951 elections, thereby closing the door to Batista's aspirations to the presidency, paved the way for his decision to seize power by force.

This turn of events was not generally anticipated in 1952. Since the beginning of the 1950s, a patriotic, social, and cultural movement gained momentum to celebrate the republic's fiftieth anniversary in May 1952. Historians, writers, geographers, and other cultural, social, and political personalities and institutions marked the occasion in a variety of ways, including the publication of important scholarly works.[1] None of the these works treated the nation's political and structural crisis of the time, although such problems were indeed recognized. In fact, a team of U.S. experts known as the Truslow Mission had concluded a study on Cuba in 1951, examining the economic, labor, social, political, educational, and cultural problems that they believed the Auténtico government should resolve to avoid a deepening of the Cuban crisis.[2] Prominent Cuban historians approached the issue from a moral point of view, declaring that the country was experiencing a crisis in patriotism.[3] They disregarded the emerging generational movement, which was opposed to corruption and critical of the scarce possibilities for mobility.

The social movements of the 1950s developed out of the March 10 coup, although they originated in nineteenth-century patriotic ideals and the hemisphere-wide renaissance that began at the end of the second decade of the twentieth century and had its strongest manifestation during the 1930 revolution. The youth who espoused these ideals of the 1930s served as a bridge generation connecting the generations of 1895 and 1950.

The proclamation of the University of Córdoba in Argentina, the origins of the renovation movement of the late 1920s, resonated across the Americas and served as a rallying call in Cuban society until the victory of the revolution. Students rebelled against corrupt university rule, political dictatorships, bossism, racial discrimination, and foreign economic control—problems that persisted through the 1930s, 1940s, and 1950s. Almost all major cities of Latin America experienced the rebellion of youth, especially Lima, Santiago de Chile, Montevideo, Bogotá, Caracas, La Paz, Quito, Asunción, Panamá, México, and Havana. Students became a vanguard of the middle classes and joined with young professionals and workers.

The reformist movements shared several goals: university autonomy, student participation in university rule, and free education. But the reform project was not limited in content and scope to educational matters. Its aim was also to forge a new moral awareness, to transform the political, economic, and social realities in which the masses lived and unite Latin American youth under its banner. Thus, its struggle against dictatorships, its emphasis on anti-imperialism, the linkages to the workers' movement, solidarity with the oppressed peoples, appeals for social justice, and demands for an effective democracy gave form and purpose to the cause.[4]

The movement was defined by José Ingenieros, Alejandro Korn, José Carlos Mariátegui, Victor Raúl Haya de la Torre, Deodoro Roca, Gabriel del Mazo, and Julio Antonio Mella.[5] It announced the birth of a new Latin America because it represented a new generation, not linked to former generations, with a different vision and other ideals.[6]

The Auténtico governments (1944–1952) dashed the hopes for social justice and progress that the new republican generation had invested in them. Dissatisfied with the existing rule, the youth turned to other ways to overcome social problems, giving new forms to the frustrated Latin American project and the objectives of a republic of justice that José Martí dreamed of. The works of thinkers like José Ingenieros, José Vasconselos, Emilio Roig de Leuchsenring, and Jorge Mañach, together with those of José Martí, became common reading. Poetry, especially modernist works by Martí, Rubén Darío, and Julián del Casal, and the political prose of Vargas Vila and others who had participated in Cuba's independence struggles nurtured the spirit of the emerging generation.

Christian and Marxist humanism further shaped the era's emphasis on the values of justice and love.

* * *

The generational movement of the 1950s steered the course of the revolution. It played the role required to achieve liberation from a regime that had violated electoral democracy and suspended the 1940 constitution. The generational vanguard that emerged in 1952 reaffirmed the *independentista* goals of Martí and the renovation movement under the banners of Ortodoxo Chibasismo. One of the groups of the 1950 generation proclaimed itself the "generation of the centennial," alluding to the 100th anniversary of Martí's birth, and sought to organize the politico-military apparatus of the insurgent wing of the Ortodoxos, explicitly considering armed actions as a means to overthrow the Batista regime.

The generation of the centennial was led by two young men, Fidel Castro and Abel Santamaría, both of them Ortodoxos. They planned the Moncada Project, structuring a political, civic, and military organization that was to play the role of a party for the "necessary war," as conceived originally in 1892 by Martí. Castro and Santamaría also established contact with Mario Muñoz from Colón, a former member of the DEU and Ortodoxo in the province of Matanzas whom they incorporated into the national leadership. Between March and May 1952, a variety of disparate patriotic revolutionary groups in the province joined together and assumed a new and separate personality as an insurgent force.

The student sector was led by the Havana FEU, which guided the Matanzas FEIM, the Student Federation of the Cárdenas Institute (Federación Estudiantil del Instituto de Cárdenas; FEIC) (which subsequently organized into the Revolutionary Directorate), and the Ortodoxo and Auténtico insurrectional forces led by the MR 26-7. The student associations of secondary schools, teachers' training schools, and arts and trades schools in Matanzas also followed the FEU's lead.

The insurgency was immediately supported by such men as José Antonio Echeverría, José Smith Comas, and Manuel del Cueto (professor at the prestigious La Progresiva school and member of Young Cuba), all from Cárdenas; Mario Muñoz from Colón; and Laudelino González from Matanzas. The latter three emerged out of Chibás's Ortodoxos. Muñoz, González, and del Cueto represented a generational continuity of the revolutionary struggle: They had fought the regime of Gerardo Machado during the 1930s, the former two as students and del Cueto as trade union leader in Cárdenas's Arrechabala Company.

Matanzas Ortodoxos Israel Tápanes and the brothers Armelio, Antonio, and Alejandro Ferrá joined what was to become the MR 26-7 cell in the Cayo Hueso neighborhood of Havana and participated in the Moncada Project.[7] In the meantime, out of the MR 26-7 cell organized in Matanzas Province by Muñoz emerged two participants in the assault on Moncada: Muñoz himself and Julio Reyes Cairo.

The March 10 coup provoked rebellion among these socially and politically heterogeneous forces derived principally from student and worker sectors.[8] Although in the minds of the original participants the use of force was fully justified as a means to dislodge Batista, the popular classes employed other, traditional means, including the general strike, demonstrations, and street actions, which often developed spontaneously. These tactics would later be appropriated by Fidel Castro and the MR 26-7 leadership to organize insurgency. Therein lay the principal methodological success of MR 26-7 in leading popular forces in the struggle to overthrow the regime, seize power, and consolidate the victory of the revolution.

Although no organized political party chose initially to confront the Batista government directly and organize workers, students, and popular classes as a whole, unity among the different political and social groups gradually evolved as they participated in demonstrations and strikes after the March 10 coup.

With regard to the labor movement, the secretary-general of the CTC, Eusebio Mujal, called for a general strike. However, when Prío and some of the ministers of the ousted Auténtico government sought political asylum in the Mexican embassy and the Auténticos failed to lead the confrontation against the illegal de facto government, Mujal decided to turn the leadership of the labor movement over to Batista's regime. Several trade unions and federations, however, balked. The sisal and textile workers' unions of Matanzas continued in the opposition until the overthrow of Batista. Their national leader, Pascasio Lineras, was arrested together with Marcos Hirigoyen of the national bus service and Calixto Sánchez of the airline workers. They had informed Mujal that they would continue to oppose Batista and support the convened general strike. In Matanzas FPTT secretary-general Julián Alemán not only led the strike but headed the insurgent workers' movement until he was murdered by the regime in April 1958.

The popular national uprising began spontaneously in the western part of the country and gathered momentum in response to a national movement that was emerging from expanding opposition to the regime imposed by force. In Havana, Matanzas, Cárdenas, Colón, Jovellanos, and smaller towns, many participated in the opposition from the very beginning and remained active until the collapse of the regime.

The first cycle of national rebellion spanned the years between 1952 and 1953. The workers pursued solutions principally through different forms of strikes in individual industries, plantations, and sectors, whereas the student movement took to the streets, organized different forms of strikes, and made public denunciations. The activities of students and workers began gradually to converge, their cooperation deepening in late 1955. The most noteworthy example of their integration was the sugar workers' strike in 1955 coordinated by the FNTA, FEU, and FEIM in the province of Matanzas. The FEU also organized a strike supported by workers in transportation, the hotel and restaurant industry, pharmacies, and banking, despite the CTC's plea not to take part in the action.[9]

All of this was the consequence of the expanding revolutionary situation during 1955. Polarization between the popular classes and the regime, particularly the police forces, intensified. A new cycle began in 1956 and lasted until the end of 1958, when most elements of the popular opposition were incorporated into the DR and the MR 26-7. Both organizations played key roles during these years in determining who would win: the Batista regime, representing the dependent and corrupt republic, or the revolution associated with independence and honesty.

* * *

The main features of the struggle that began within the student sectors of the capital and Matanzas in 1952 were the call to the people to reject Batista's constitutional statutes, support for the restoration of the 1940 constitution, and the use of symbolic dates commemorating past patriotic struggles to motivate participants to challenge the regime. As the movement evolved, the armed forces and students clashed, and the Ortodoxo and Auténtico youth resorted to revolutionary violence to counteract state violence.

The morning of March 10, 1952, the FEU voted to "strike indefinitely and actively support and defend civilian power." The strike reached Matanzas through the FEIM and other student associations.

Students hung banners with anti-Batista slogans at the University of Havana and the Matanzas Institute and used the public address systems to denounce the coup. A manifesto repudiating the coup was signed by, among others, FEU leaders Alvaro Barba and José Antonio Echeverría. The FEIM also distributed a leaflet addressed to "the people" condemning the coup and on March 20 issued a manifesto signed by the Youth Directorate of Matanzas affirming its opposition to the coup.[10]

Ortodoxo and the Ortodoxo Youth leaders and legislators organized several demonstrations. As leader of the Ortodoxo Youth, lawyer Fidel Castro on March 15 sent a letter to Batista predicting that the coup would mean corruption, theft, torture, and death for Cuba and that the reaction of the people would force him from power. Several days later (March 24) Castro introduced a brief before the constitutional guarantees court charging the regime with unconstitutionality. At the same time, he denounced Batista in Havana's lower court for having violated six articles of the Social Defense Code, for which he said Batista deserved more than 100 years in jail. Castro argued that instead of a nation ruled by justice and order, there was abuse and brutality.[11]

At the same time, a group of lawmakers led by Ortodoxos Luis Orlando Rodríguez, a former president of the FEU; Pelayo Cuervo; and Manuel Bisbé were shot at by soldiers protecting the capitol when they attempted to enter to perform their duties as legislators. The Ortodoxo leadership also addressed the UN secretary-general and the Organization of American States (OAS) denouncing the coup as a violation of the principles set forth by the charters of these organizations.[12] In April the FEU summoned students, workers, and people at large to the "constitution's funeral" at the University of Havana. After symbolically burying a copy of the 1940 constitution, "murdered by Batista," the protestors held a mass demonstration.

The regime responded. Several students were taken to police stations and brutally beaten. In court those charged with conspiracy against the state were further abused, state security forces harassing and intimidating judicial powers and even jailing defense lawyers.[13]

In the month after the coup, repression against the opposition increased in Havana and Matanzas, part of expanding government violence across the island. Student struggles intensified from early April to late May 1952 on the occasion of the fiftieth anniversary of the republic. In Matanzas students were backed by the popular sector in the mobilizations of May 8, the anniversary of the death of nationalist leader Antonio Guiteras and thus an important date for supporters of rebellion against Batista's regime. To commemorate the date, the Matanzas FEIM and the rayon workers' trade union agreed to organize a march to the site of Guiteras's murder. The associations of the secondary schools, teachers' training schools, and arts and trades schools also participated in the march.

During these months José Antonio Echeverría, Fructuoso Rodríguez, and other FEU leaders visited Matanzas Province several times to take part in demonstrations and mass rallies organized by the FEIM, FEIC, and various student associations and held in the cities of Matanzas, Jovellanos, Colón, and Cárdenas. Mario Muñoz, chief of MR 26-7 in Matanzas and member of the national leadership, helped organize rallies in Matanzas cities and towns. Muñoz also met with FEIM leaders in their Matanzas offices and planned the mobilization of several political and social sectors.

These events had national repercussions. In Havana a symbolic coffin draped with the Cuban flag was to be carried from the university, past La Punta (the site where medical students were accused of anti-Spanish slander and executed by the colonial government in 1871), to the presidential palace, concluding the march at José Martí's statue in the central park. When the regime learned of the plan, it mobilized the police. The government arrested several leaders of FEU, taking them to the military station of Camp Columbia.

Neither repression nor persuasion deterred students. The demonstration proceeded as planned. The coffin was guarded by police cars. A rally was improvised in the Rincón Martiano and another next to the statue at the main entrance to the university. "Bloc of Young Cuban Students" was the heading used on the obituary published and signed by a newly formed committee calling for the participation of workers, students, and all freedom-loving people. The influence of the 1930 Directorate had reemerged within the student movement.

While all these events were taking place in Havana, the army in Matanzas encircled Colón Park on May 19 but was unable to stop the demonstrations. The rally ended with cries of "Down with Batista!" and "Long live the revolution!" One student was injured in the clash with soldiers.[14]

The mobilization of all sectors in support of the 1940 constitution created a climate favorable to advancing conditions for rebellion. Youth distributed hundreds of leaflets against the government with the motto "FEU—Constitutional Invasion" and calling on the people to attend rallies on June 10, 12 and 14, 1952. The courts opened cases against FEU leader Echeverría and others, charging them with inciting public disorder.[15]

In June the FEU called for Batista's resignation and the selection of an FEU-appointed provisional president, a political formula similar to that of the 1930 Student Directorate. On November 27, the anniversary of the execution of the medical students in 1871, the FEIM convened a rally by the house where Carlos Verdugo, one of the students, had lived, near the Goicuría Garrison in Matanzas. In December FEU leaders and people of Matanzas marched across the city, shouting, "Down with the dictatorship!" and "Down with Batista!"[16]

Groups of Ortodoxo Matanzas professionals began to unite, giving lectures on the situation in Cuba. Manifestos distributed to the population by supporters of insurgency charged Batista with a series of murders and cited the destruction of radio stations and the closing of dailies as methods of violence and terror Batista had used since 1934.[17]

In early 1953 two pivotal events occurred: the vandalization of Julio Antonio Mella's bust at the University of Havana on January 8 and a torchlight demonstration on January 28. Students took to the streets and police units attacked. One medical student, Rubén Batista, was seriously wounded and later died.

In response, the FEIM organized several rallies to condemn the regime's actions. The students took over the buildings of the institute of secondary education and the business school, where another confrontation with police forces took place. Matanzas teachers' training school was also occupied as part of this action. Two student groups participated, one inside the building and the other outside. The latter group was arrested by the police but subsequently escaped in the confusion.[18]

On the first anniversary of the March 10 coup, demonstrations led to the arrest and wounding of students at the University of Havana and several provincial towns and cities, including the city of Matanzas. On May 4, 1953, the highly rated television program "University of the Airwaves" was interrupted during a lecture by Elías Entralgo. The police forcibly entered the studio, provoking a clash with the revolutionaries. The vice president of the law student association, Armando Hart Dávalos, and Faustino Pérez of the school of medicine participated in that action.

* * *

While the student sector confronted the regime through street actions and improvised rallies, the revolutionary movement was being secretly organized as a political-military structure. Cells were established in Matanzas and the rest of the west among workers, professionals, and students. This wide social base gave the movement the possibility of playing the role of a party in guiding a popular movement. The MNR was not as influential in Matanzas as it was elsewhere on the island, although several Matanzas Auténtico and Ortodoxo revolutionaries were members.

Between 1952 and July 1953, the national leadership of the revolutionary organization concentrated on developing the political-military structure and training its members in strict secrecy. During 1952–1953 the members of the movement participated in few public activities. They were present only at the torchlight parade on January 28, 1953, which signaled the debut of the centennial generation as a vanguard that would lead the people along the path of rebellion rather than leaving them to depend on elections as a form of opposition struggle.

On July 26, 1953, 165 youth, backed by 3,000 organized fighters in the western provinces and led by Fidel Castro and Abel Santamaría, attacked the garrisons of Santiago de Cuba and Bayamo to begin a nationwide armed uprising. Although they were militarily defeated, they proved that it was possible to carry out underground actions without the knowledge of the repressive government agencies and to enter an army post by surprise. The most important short-term achievement was that as of that moment and during the trials of the Moncada assailants, the movement came into full public view as a new political, civic, and military force with a program of economic, political, cultural, and social reform demanded by the Cuban people. The Moncada Project initiated the independentist process of the revolution and gave a name to the emerging political force.

Of the many participants from Matanzas Province, Mario Muñoz was murdered at Moncada. The Matanzas daily *El Imparcial* made his assassination known on July 28 and indentified Muñoz as "one of the most prestigious doctors" of the province, an outstanding president of the Society Club (Sociedad Liceo), and dean of the municipal college of Colón.[19]

Repression worsened throughout the province after July, mainly in the provincial capital and in Colón, Jovellanos, Cárdenas, and Unión de Reyes, where more than 180 people were arrested and tried for antigovernment acts, sabotage, burning sugarcane fields, antigovernment propaganda, and crimes against state powers. All FEIM leaders were arrested in August and September 1953, taken to the Goicuría garrison, interrogated by the regimental intelligence unit, and subsequently tried by the lower court.

Classes at the Cárdenas Institute resumed on September 19. The government used that opportunity to place police guards inside the school. A few days later, when the trials against the attackers of the Moncada barracks began, government repression, previously confined to the eastern provinces, expanded to the western end of the island. In late September 400 policemen attacked the University of Havana, openly violating its autonomy. The police disarmed the university security guards, searched faculty offices and other premises, and forced patients of Calixto García Hospital to leave their beds and line up in the yard. When the police operations were over, twelve people had been arrested and sent to prison at La Cabaña fortress.

As part of the national government campaign, the Matanzas army command also attacked students and workers. The beginning of the trial against the Moncada assailants coincided with the expiration date of the institute's registration period. School officials kept FEIM leaders from enrolling in classes in order to prevent daily and direct contact between the main youth leaders and the students. The plan was carried out with police support, a twenty-four-hour guard being stationed in the school. A number of the FEIM leaders were arrested and tried in Matanzas. Although school officials and other Batista authorities charged them with agitation, district attorney Mario Fernández defended them and urged their acquittal. Many of their supporters tried to attend the trial but were ejected from the courtroom.

Some of the defendants were subsequently acquitted. Seven, including Juan Rivero Mechoso, the president of the FEIM, were sentenced to prison terms. Once the trial ended, the students involved were expelled from the institute. Many enrolled in other schools and continued their work among students, thereby strengthening the patriotic network of insurrectional struggles against the Batista regime.[20]

Rather than stifling student opposition, the government's actions encouraged it. Reaction against government political-military measures came immediately. Several leaders of the FEIM and the teachers' training school released a statement denouncing government repression; they received the support of José Smith Comas, leader of the FEIC, and other associations of Matanzas.

Among the many cases brought to trial by the police in Matanzas in 1953 were those of several groups implicated in the attack against the Moncada garrison and the distribution of subversive antigovernment propaganda. These documents were seized, according to *El*

Imparcial, in "all towns of Matanzas Province," including Juan Gualberto Gómez and Jagüey.[21]

In 1954 José Antonio Echeverría from Cárdenas was elected president of the FEU at the University of Havana. An advocate of armed opposition against the Batista regime, he defined the political posture of the student movement. In 1955 Echeverría declared at a press conference that one of his goals as head of the FEU was to commit the student movement to the people and cultural development. For that reason, they would set up the Rafael Trejo People's University and the Rubén Batista Literacy Campaign. Another goal was to organize an international congress aimed at developing ideological ties among Latin American university students. He stressed the importance of spurring activism among all Cuban youth who longed for freedom and fighting for democracy in the face of the blindness of all political parties. Hopes for a democratic-revolutionary project rested in the struggle of youth not compromised by political opportunism.[22]

During early 1955, police-student confrontations increased, as did the reciprocal support between workers and students in strikes and demonstrations. The tactic of staging protests to coincide with the dates of past revolutionary events further consecrated the occasions as nationalist symbols. Several rallies were held in May 1955 on the twentieth anniversary of the assassination of Antonio Guiteras. At the Matanzas rally attended by José Antonio Echeverría, police fired upon the demonstrators and attacked them with blackjacks. The student movement increasingly turned into armed struggle.

* * *

The president of the FEU led the amnesty movement on behalf of the Moncada prisoners, who had been excluded from a proposed May 15 amnesty decree. When Fidel Castro and the other assailants were released from the Isle of Pines prison on May 15, 1955, Echeverría traveled to the Havana railroad station to welcome them. The first personal meeting between Echeverría and Castro was on May 17, when Echeverría asked Castro to deliver the closing speech at a May 20 rally.[23] When the students welcomed the revolutionaries to the university, the police surrounded the campus, closed traffic by shooting at anyone who came near, and interrupted the power supply. That night people spoke under the light of kerosene lamps and paid tribute to "the martyrs and heroes of Moncada."[24]

The regime did not let up, aware that revolutionary forces across the island, under the leadership of Castro and Echeverría, were growing in number. The government also kept strict control, both in Cuba and the United States, over all activities of the Auténticos, especially Carlos Prío Socarrás. In June the regime charged Prío with organizing terrorist actions from Miami and plotting to overthrow the Cuban government; U.S. authorities detained Prío for a time. The government named FEU leaders Francisco Rodríguez, Alvaro Barba, and Raúl Castro as well as other revolutionaries as co-conspirators. A few days later FEU leader Juan Pedro Carbó Serviá was arrested for placing a bomb at the Infanta Theater. Carbó was released during the trial for lack of evidence. At a press conference the following month, the FEU and the university council protested the police search of the university under the pretext of seeking concealed weapons.[25]

One of the most important events in the revolutionary process occurred on July 7. Fidel Castro left for Mexico to prepare, direct, and train the MR 26-7 for the expedition that would later land on the southern coast of Oriente. The plans the MR 26-7 drew up from 1955 to 1956 were similar to those of the Moncada project: to conduct an insurrection based on armed struggle combined with direct antigovernment acts, sabotage, and guerrilla warfare, with the support of a general strike. The change was in the military structures, guerrilla tactics having been added to urban commando actions. The provincial commands of the MR 26-7 were to launch the insurrection while the expeditionary forces trained in Mexico reached the Sierra Maestra. While Castro and the MR 26-7 prepared the expeditionary landing, Echeverría led the student movement as a whole to organize the Revolutionary Directorate of the 1950s. At the same time, Antonio López, the MR 26-7 delegate, began organizing the youth movement into youth action and sabotage brigades and agitation, propaganda, and finance cells.

Police harassment against the student sector mounted. Two days after Castro went into exile, police forces again searched the university without legal authorization, ransacking offices and destroying furniture and documents. The government claimed to have seized several rifles and ammunition belonging to conspirators of an insurrectional movement based at the university. They charged that the conspiracy was led by Castro and Echeverría. The FEU brought criminal charges against the chief of police for violating the autonomy of the university and declared that this abuse was part of a previously announced plan by Minister of the Interior Santiago Rey to harass student leaders.

FEU leaders agreed to celebrate the second anniversary of the Moncada attack by holding a meeting at the university on July 26. Fructuoso Rodríguez spoke and Echeverría presided over the gathering, which took place in the Salón de Mártires (Salon of Martyrs). Once again the police encircled the campus and detoured traffic; a clash between students and police was unavoidable.

Extremely important events occurred over the summer. A number of pro-insurrection militants and leaders, made up mainly of elements of the revolutionary youth movement, joined the MR 26-7. With their incorporation into the organization in June–August 1955, the MR 26-7 became a stronger political-military structure and assumed the role of a "party for war" to guide the people's movement in Cuba, in exile, and among Cuban émigrés. Fidel Castro and the MR 26-7 opposed the electoral path to revolution, believing instead that it was necessary to establish a young party to make the insurgency a reality, since times were "revolutionary, not political."[26]

Meanwhile, Echeverría's civic appeal reached the public through the press and *Bohemia* magazine, not as a party message but as a patriotic message. The FEU was determined to fulfill a duty inherited from "the great martyrs and guides of the students and the nation: Julio Antonio Mella, Rafael Trejo, Antonio Guiteras, Eddy Chibás, Ramiro Valdés Daussá" and from the 1923 university reform, when the José Martí People's University had gathered students and workers for "a better Cuba." History seemed to repeat itself in the actions of these youths who spoke of the future "on behalf of that glorious past."[27]

In November 1956 the Society of Friends of the Republic (Sociedad de Amigos de la República; SAR) convened a meeting of the opposition. Among those who attended were Grau San Martín, Carlos Prío, Raúl Chibás, Amalio Fiallo, José Pardo Llada, Juan Marinello, and José Antonio Echeverría.[28]

In fact, the FEU was increasingly opting for the insurrectional path, rejecting elections and opposing civic dialogue. Serious clashes between students and the police occurred in November–December 1955 beginning in Santiago de Cuba on November 27. Several students disappeared, and others were either made prisoners or wounded. The following day the FEU called for a forty-eight-hour strike to support the students of Oriente. On November 29 a demonstration at the Vedado Institute resulted in the arrest of

Echeverría and other student leaders. Other demonstrations were held in Havana, Matanzas, Artemisa, Santa Clara, Camagüey, Santiago de Cuba, Holguín, and Manzanillo.[29] Participants in the protests across the island carried Cuban flags and posters against the regime, leading to arrests and injuries.[30]

In Havana the demonstration began with a march to the residence of Colonel Cosme de la Torriente, head of the SAR, to deliver a letter suggesting the stance the opposition should adopt. In the subsequent street battle, Echeverría, his brother Alfredo, and Fructuoso Rodríguez, as well as several policemen, were seriously wounded. Classes at the University of Havana and the secondary education institutes were suspended, and Minister of the Interior Santiago Rey banned all public meetings. The chief of police, Rafael Salas Cañizares, ordered the rector of the University of Havana to expel "communists and troublesome elements," in keeping with the regime's campaign of labeling the insurgent democratic-revolutionary movement as leftist.

The regime arrested some twenty students for jumping onto the field of Cerro Stadium during a baseball game, carrying banners denouncing the government. Echeverría was charged with public disorder and Fructuoso Rodríguez with assault with a firearm.

On December 5, the eve of the anniversary of the death of nineteenth-century independence leader General Antonio Maceo, Camilo Cienfuegos, Juan Pedro Carbó Serviá, and other students were wounded in Havana while they were returning to the university after placing a wreath on Maceo's monument. The FEIM organized the December 7 demonstration in Matanzas with the participation of all the student associations. A debate on the student-police clashes took place in the Cuban house of representatives the next day. The opposition maintained that the public decried police aggression against the students and that the regime was not interested in peace and national harmony. Government legislators insisted that the incidents were part of a scheme to provoke insurrection.

Student Manuel Cervantes was killed during the December 7 confrontations in Ciego de Avila. The following day the FEU convened a rally. When they were preparing to take a symbolic coffin to Havana's Maceo Park, police forces disbanded the march, resulting in widespread injury. In a response, the student federation called for a five-minute, national work stoppage on December 14. The general-secretary of the CTC, Eusebio Mujal, declared that no agreement had been reached concerning the five minutes of silence. Despite this lack of a united front and a lack of organization, the transportation, railroad, sugar, tobacco, hotel-restaurant, pharmaceutical, beer, cigarette, telephone, and banking trade unions supported the FEU's appeal for a work stoppage to demonstrate worker solidarity with the students. For its part, the SAR issued a lengthy statement evaluating the attitude of the government, criticizing the police for confronting students, and demanding the release of teachers, students, and other arrested citizens.

Pressure mounted and the courts were forced to release leaders Echeverría, his brother Alfredo, Fructuoso Rodríguez, and Osmel Francis. During the same period, Echeverría met with the FNTA leaders to support the December 1955 general strike to protest a conflict between the government and plantation owners over nonpayment of the previous harvest's sugar bonus. FEU leaders went to various regions in Matanzas to organize the strike movement, which expanded to all sugar mills of the province under the leadership of Conrado Rodríguez and Conrado Bécquer, the principal representatives of the FNTA at the national level.

In an interview published in *Carteles* in January 1956, Echeverría said that despite the haste in organizing the national work stoppage, it had been a complete success, "a true victory" for both the working class and the students. Affirming that students and workers were "struggling together for truth and liberty," Echeverría predicted that worker-student solidarity would grow.[31] *Bohemia* magazine published an editorial identifying Cuban students as determined and resolute, "aware of themselves and what surrounds them," understanding that their presence in the country's life would not be limited to a "mere change of name in the regime" but to the "most profound changes in the social structure" of the Cuban nation.[32]

The year 1956 began with further confrontations between opposition sectors and the government. The significant difference in 1956 was that the MR 26-7 participated in mobilizations as an organized force. On January 28—one of the most important symbolic dates for the Cuban youth movement, the anniversary of the birth of José Martí—the FEU organized a national mobilization that was attended by students at large and the MR 26-7 youth action and sabotage brigade members. Riots took place in Havana's Central Park when the police tried to prevent students from placing a wreath on the Martí monument. Several leaders of the FEU, including Echeverría, were beaten and arrested. Similar events took place in Cárdenas, Santa Clara, Camagüey, Guantánamo, and Santiago de Cuba. A similar clash occurred several weeks later in a demonstration at the site where Rubén Batista was killed; once again police fired on the students.

In a speech at the great hall of the University of Havana on February 24, 1956, Echeverría for the first time publicly referred to the establishment of the DR sponsored by FEU. The DR's programmatic and ideological "Manifesto to the People of Cuba" stated that insurrection was the only way to obtain liberty "because of the inefficacy of outdated political parties and the unity of students and workers not subjected to [CTCV general-secretary] Mujal's Batista-type policies."[33]

The attack on the provincial regimental headquarters in Matanzas in April 1956 was the most significant action by Auténtico elements. The army command had apparently been informed of the plot, and most of the 100 members of the Auténtico commando squad died in the action; others were subsequently tracked down and killed, and several escaped to Mexico. The impact of these events, however, was so serious that the government once again suspended constitutional guarantees and imposed censorship of the media.

With close contacts in Matanzas Province, Echeverría was forced to go underground. In August 1956 he left the country to represent Cuba at two students congresses. Once the Latin American Congress of Santiago de Chile ended and after visiting other nations of South and Central America, he traveled to Mexico to meet with Fidel Castro. The meeting lasted several days, during which the two drafted and signed the "Mexico letter" declaring the unity of the MR 26-7 and the FEU, the two most militant organizations of the antigovernment insurgency. Calling their agreement a letter instead of a pact, a term used by the old political parties, they stated that both organizations would join in efforts to overthrow the Batista government and carry out the revolution. Castro and Echeverría considered the social and political conditions appropriate to issue a call for insurrection backed by a general strike across the island. Both leaders believed that the revolution would triumph without compromises, based on a program of social justice, liberty, democracy, respect for just laws, and recognition of the full dignity of all Cubans.

The document was made public in Cuba in early September. Reactions to the letter, both from the regime and from sectors of the opposition and from within some groups at the University of Havana, were openly hostile. For this reason, FEU's leaders called a meeting, and the majority of the membership ratified Echeverría's action. The leadership also agreed to publish a declaration in support of the Mexico letter in which the new generation represented in the DR and the MR 26-7 committed themselves to "overthrow the tyranny and carry on the revolution" and to oppose the so-called civic dialogue. The document, signed by Fructuoso Rodríguez as FEU president and Juan Nuiry as secretary-general, proclaimed the need to achieve the unity of all revolutionary groups to confront the "dictatorship" and called the Mexico declaration the first fruit of such efforts by the DR, established and encouraged by the FEU.

Echeverría traveled to Miami to meet with Rodríguez and Nuiry, who informed him of the reaction to the Mexico letter. All three subsequently left for Mexico to discuss strategy with Castro. Castro explained to the FEU leaders the objectives of the joint actions. Both fields of action were clearly defined at a national level. The MR 26-7 armed insurgent forces would land and open a guerrilla front while the FEU and the DR promoted actions that, together with those of the MR 26-7's underground structure, would provoke armed urban insurrection and give way to the revolutionary general strike. The purpose was to disperse the regime's forces around different regions of the country, thereby weakening the offensive capacity of the army against the expeditionary group at the landing site.[34]

The FEU leaders left for Miami in mid-October 1956. There they exchanged views before departing for Cuba and prepared their plans to avoid being arrested on arrival at the Rancho Boyeros airport in Havana. They knew that the Congress of the Inter-American Press Association, led by Julis Dubois, was being held in Havana. The regime was trying to project an image of legality to the rest of the world, covering up its constant suspensions of constitutional guarantees and its press censorship. Under the circumstances the FEU leaders decided to arrive in Cuba in two groups: Rodríguez and Nuiry first, then Echeverría and the rest of the group.

In order to gain legal entrance to Cuba, Fructuoso and Nuiry announced their arrival to Inter-American Press Association delegations, convened the Cuban media, and mobilized the students to welcome them at the airport. The group implemented the same plan for Echeverría's return on October 24, and a large crowd of reporters, photographers, and students greeted him on his arrival. Faure Chomón, a leader of the DR who was wanted by the government, was the only one to travel clandestinely.

Within days after Echeverría returned to Cuba, Colonel Antonio Blanco Rico, head of the SIM, was assassinated. Two days later national police chief brigadier Rafael Salas Cañizares and his men, disregarding diplomatic immunity, invaded the Haitian embassy in Havana and killed a group of young revolutionaries. Salas Cañizares was wounded in the attack and died forty-eight hours later.

Pro-government groups charged that *fidelistas* and the FEU were organizing a terrorist campaign in Mexico. When FEU leaders arrived in Cuba, they declared that there was already "absolute unity among revolutionary forces," who accepted Fidel Castro's leadership.[35] In the daily *Ataja*, Fulgencio Batista said that he had reports from SIM and police chiefs that several attacks were being organized against civilian and military members of the regime and that the insurrectionists were trying to show the inter-American press that there was no peace or democracy in Cuba.

A national student demonstration against the regime took place on November 27, 1956. It was the largest street confrontation with police forces, the mobilization spreading to all provinces despite government threats and the terror unleashed by the police. The militancy of the student sector was uncontainable and uncontrollable. More than 600 students marched from the University of Havana, and similar protests occurred in Matanzas, Santiago de Cuba, Guantánamo, and Santa Clara. As a result, a movement developed across the island calling for a general student strike. Havana's university closed its doors from November 1956 until January 1959. In that period, only religious and private schools continued their academic activities uninterrupted, though in many cases they, too, supported the student insurrectional movement. This was the beginning of the "necessary war" in Cuba.

Actions and sabotage increased through early 1957. By March 1957 the DR had enough weapons to carry out a significant action and attacked the presidential palace and the Radio Reloj station in an attempt to provoke a people's rebellion. José Antonio Echeverría died in that action. The abortive assault on the presidential palace, and especially the deaths of the principal student leaders, announced the collapse of the FEU as an important revolutionary group in the armed struggle against the Batista government. What remained of the leaders and followers within the FEU dispersed into other revolutionary organizations.

In late 1957 Nuiry, vice president of the FEU, went to the Sierra Maestra; his meeting with Castro "was in itself a reaffirmation of the positions maintained by both organizations," based on the agreed principle "that the leadership of the highest student body joined the vanguard of the struggle." Nuiry conveyed "the main agreement: that the leadership of the student movement was joining the rebel army and its general command."[36]

The kind of sabotage used by the liberation army of the nineteenth century (in particular, the burning of sugarcane fields) reemerged in the people's struggle against the Batista government immediately after March 1952. Strikes, worker-student demonstrations, and street actions rounded out their tactics. When these events began, there was no articulated insurrectional organization as such, but a structure evolved in the western portion of the nation a few weeks after the coup d'état.

From the earliest hours of the March coup, the FEU assumed the role of the main opposition in Havana and rushed to the palace expecting President Prío to issue weapons to them. A few days later, Fidel Castro issued a statement denouncing Batista. He maintained that the seizure of power was not a "revolution" but a blow. One of his greatest merits was his understanding of the need to organize a revolutionary structure as a people's instrument of struggle, so that all classes could participate in overthrowing the regime.

Within the generation of 1950, two main tendencies emerged. In one the students carried forward the ideals of anti-imperialist revolution of the 1930 DEU and Martí. The other involved a popular vanguard that initially defined itself as the "centennial generation," made up of different social sectors and classes who upheld the independentist ideals of Julio Antonio Mella, Antonio Guiteras, Eduardo Chibás, and José Martí and recognized the need to organize a new liberation army to fight for a just and democratic republic.

3

The Political Economy of the Batista Government

The restrictive sugar harvest policies during 1952–1958 hurt agro-industrial workers and Cuba's rural economy in general. In December 1952 Ortodoxo leader Pelayo Cuervo denounced Batista's sugar policy, blaming that policy for the poverty and hunger of large sectors of the population. Writer Samuel Feijóo bemoaned the desperate situation of 42,000 small farmers doomed to disappear as a result of government policies.[1]

In Matanzas Province, friction among industrialists, factory workers, farmers, and agricultural workers came about with the displacement of workers, depressed wages, salary arrears, and excess production. This was especially true in the sugar, textiles, and sisal industries, producing tensions that reached their peak in late September 1952.

The problems of sugar workers were similar to those of sisal workers, public employees, and service workers. Sisal workers from Mariel, Pinar del Río, to Nuevitas, Camagüey, went on strike to protest salary reductions. In late 1952, 30,000 textile workers went on strike in support of sisal workers, resulting in the arrest of hundreds.[2] The Federation of Textile Workers of Matanzas (Federación de Trabajadores Textiles de Matanzas), under the leadership of Ortodoxo Julián Alemán, created a workers' committee in July 1953 to implement a program to defend their gains and avoid wage cuts and layoffs. Economic conflict originated in the debate concerning the enforcement of Decree 2144, which authorized the importation of tariff-free synthetic fibers in order to provide workers with raw material during shortages of domestically produced natural fibers, thus avoiding layoffs. The Confederation of Owners of Cuba (Confederación Patronal de Cuba) was founded in September 1953 to deal with workers' demands.

Matanzas plantation owners were constantly cutting wages and in October 1953 took action that negatively affected preharvest repair works in several sugar mills.

Deteriorating conditions manifested themselves not only in the economic field as a result of conflict between capital and labor but also in the political-military sphere, since police forces had to confront workers in labor conflicts. The army continued to repress labor protests against employers, causing sugar workers to burn more sugarcane fields and prompting other forms of sabotage that instigated yet another round of repression. The regime described the protection of sugar mills and roadblocks as an "efficient action of the army" and repeatedly urged the peaceful solution of the labor disputes.[3]

Confrontations involving business interests, plantation owners, *colonos* (sugar farmers), and sugar workers sharpened in 1954. In January in the region of Colón, the *colonos* of the España sugar mill protested because labor leaders of the Tinguaro mill had agreed to begin the harvest without first liquidating the payments for the previous harvest.

Conflicts arose not only between sugar industrialists and factory workers but also among *colonos* and rural workers. In April 1954 the police arrested Domingo Casanova Orihuela, provincial leader of the FNTA, and Reynaldo Domínguez, secretary-general of the trade union, for ordering workers of the Cuba sugar mill not to start milling until *colonos* paid their debts to the agricultural workers. The mill administrator charged that some half a million tons of sugarcane had not been ground.[4]

Public officials and civil servants were also affected by government measures. From the outset 1954 was characterized by increased layoffs, beginning with the suspension of 78 employees in the Ministry of the Interior. In answering questions from journalists, Minister Ramón O. Hermida acknowledged "with full candor" that "as a result of the layoffs, not one single employee of the overthrown [Prío] regime will remain."[5] An official January resolution announced a 10 percent wage cut for teachers, professors, and employees of the Ministry of Education. The Havana college of education protested and argued that while the pope had appealed for a wage increase, the government enacted cuts.[6] The Association of Landowners (Asociación de Hacendados) declared itself in permanent session and threatened to suspend the harvest because of wage problems, thus deepening tensions.[7]

State control over CTC leadership became increasingly obvious. Vicente Martínez, law inspector of the Labor Ministry, informed bank workers' leaders in Las Villas that they could not continue to head the trade union "since a government appointee had to be there." José Mármol Díaz, secretary-general of the union, opposed the measure, was arrested, subsequently disappeared, and was later found dead in Palmira, Las Villas.[8]

In February 1954 the government debated budgetary adjustments. Some believed it was necessary to balance expenditures through taxes or revenues; others favored continuing government economic functions, even though that could imply a continued deficit.[9] In the same week, the Cuban Electric Power Company asked the Central Utilities Council to suspend the 45 percent gas rate reduction that had benefited the population through a decree passed by the 1933 revolutionary government.[10]

On March 2 an incident occurred in the town of Guamacaro that deepened the conflict between Compañía Operadora Canimar and the Limones sugar mill workers. The problem became so serious that President Fulgencio Batista was forced to intervene. In the conciliatory meeting at the Ministry of Labor, the enterprise argued lack of cost-effectiveness of the business, while the workers asked that the sugar mill be turned over to the University of Havana so that the state would become responsible for its operation to avoid labor cuts. The ministry ordered the workers to return to their jobs and that the labor conditions that had existed during the 1953 harvest be maintained.

During early 1954 the government attempted to implement the aspect of the Truslow Mission Plan related to compensated layoffs. The document, presented to the CTC, argued that employers could lay off workers without considering their records "through a simple warning and a one-month economic compensation per year of service."[11]

A 5 percent cut in export quotas was announced in May for a group of countries that were members of the International Sugar Agreement, which represented an attempt to regulate international sugar trade in the world market through the creation of export quotas and the regulation of production of participating countries. The twenty-four signatory nations agreed to adjust sugar production in their territories for the duration of the agreement, a total of five years. When added to the 15 percent cut imposed in 1954, this new cut meant a 20 percent cut in London's basic quotas. The readjustment was not general, since Britain maintained its privileges; Cuba had to bear most of the restriction. It also meant that Cuba's 2.2-million-ton quota would be reduced to 1.8 million tons. The most significant aspect was that the cut had strong support from the sugar planters, as it represented a "price increase game" of which they were the beneficiaries.[12]

In May, as the election season approached, the government once again started a new wave of layoffs. Public servants were released and electoral agents loyal to the regime were appointed as their replacements. Five pro-government political parties participated in the scheme.[13]

By midyear the conflict in the Limones sugar mill deepened. Despite the agreements the company and the government had reached earlier that year, in November 1954 the enterprise refused to complete certain repairs in time. Trade union leaders denounced the move, claiming that with the stoppage of the mill hundreds of workers would lose their jobs and suffer serious economic hardship. In the Puerto and Zorrilla sugar mills in Colón, employers similarly failed to start repairs, thus idling hundreds of workers. Labor leaders convened a meeting in November 1954 in Limonar to protest the inactivity of the Limones sugar mill. The upper classes were mobilized as well, for if repairs were not carried out and the sugar mill could not operate, the *colonos* might transfer their quotas to other sugar mills.

Layoffs and wage cuts during November 1954 increased to the point that the sugar conflict expanded to the U.S.-owned Cuban Consolidated Railroad with a layoff of 1,220 workers and a 20 percent wage cut for employees. These measures provoked massive opposition, particularly from the commercial and industrial sectors, and seriously affected Matanzas, although Camagüey Province bore the brunt, with 900 layoffs. The president of Consolidated Railroad declared that U.S. shareholders were not obtaining profits but had "shown great faith in Cuba's future" and had insisted that "the enterprise's management remain in Cuban hands."[14]

In 1954 and early 1955, a 7.31 percent wage cut for sugar workers and the subsequent loss of $20 million were made public. Meanwhile, Consolidated Railroad declared that wages would be paid on a prorated basis, since it lacked the funds to pay them in full.[15]

Conflict increased in February 1955, forecasting a change in the measures that had affected different sectors of the population. The Association of *Colonos* (Asociación de Colonos), claiming to represent 70,000 sugar farmers, complained that many plantation owners were not complying with harvest payments.[16] This delay coincided with moves on the part of plantation owners, who hoped to modify Decree 805, which guaranteed payment for the farmers' sugarcane.[17]

The crisis sharpened to such an extent that all means were used to solve the problem, without making anything public. In February Batista, vice president Andrés Domingo Morales del Castillo, and the ministers of labor, finance, transportation, and agriculture met with employers and labor representatives. After meeting with Generals Tabernilla and Salas Cañizares and the chief of military intelligence and investigation services, Batista reported to the press that they had discussed "disturbing activities originating in Miami to sabotage the harvest and agitate workers and assassination attempts against the president-elect."[18]

Conditions finally led to the collapse of the CTC, its locals, and its trade unions. Many labor leaders opposed the pro-government position of the CTC secretary-general, who responded more to the interests of employers than to those of the workers. Congressman and general-subsecretary of the FNTA Conrado Bécquer, despite his parliamentary immunity, was arrested in Jovellanos and kept under custody in the rural guard's garrison. He declared that the rural guard had beaten workers of the Soledad sugar mill of Jovellanos with their machetes. Because of the scandal, the Cuban legislature condemned Bécquer's arrest during a closed session.[19]

In April 1955 seventeen U.S. congressmen from sugar-producing states introduced a bill proposing higher sugar quotas for those states at the expense of the quotas of Cuba and other nations. The president of the Cuban *colonos'* association said the possible change in the U.S. sugar law posed a serious threat to the island's sugar producers.

During the same period, a CTC delegation to the congress of the Inter-American Regional Organization of Workers (Organización Regional Interamericana de Trabajadores; ORIT) stated that foreign capital, especially U.S. capital, should invest in Cuba to create new income sources and mitigate unemployment.[20] Within the framework of sugar policy, a survey sponsored by the Cuban Sugar Stabilization Institute (Instituto Cubano de Estabilización del Azucár; ICEA) showed that Cuba's annual imports of agricultural and manufactured goods benefited more than 18,000 companies and plants in 1,800 U.S. communities.

At that time the National Finance Corporation (Financiera Nacional) contributed $10 million to the expansion of the Cuban Electric Power Company.[21] Many Cuban capitalists from the nonsugar

sector were nationalists, leading many of them to join the opposition and avoid participation in the projects of Batista's regime.
It was within this context that the Matanzas workers' movement in mid-1955 created a new association within the CTC itself
and operated in conjunction with trade unions and provincial and
national underground leaderships. This militant labor movement
established links with different Ortodoxo and Auténtico groups and
with the MR 26-7 workers' sections, which promoted a revolutionary general strike in support of armed struggle. To its goals of overthrowing the regime that was undermining the nation's economic
development, the workers' sections added the goal of liberating the
country. While the insurrectional workers' organization was being
formed, Matanzas threatened to declare itself a "paralyzed city" because of the stoppage of textile plants as a result of worker layoffs.[22]

The agroindustrial problems that had been confounding the
government since the first half of the year continued to worsen in
May and June. A trade union delegation led by Eusebio Mujal went
to Washington in May to request U.S. trade union support in fighting sugar quota cuts.[23]

The following month witnessed increased labor conflicts in the
Cuban Railroad Company, where workers went on strike, and
other workers threatened to support them. The CTC responded
simply by declaring that nobody could go on strike until the executive committee made the necessary arrangements. The government issued an ultimatum threatening to fire strikers if they refused
to return to work.

The pro-government CTC general-secretary was losing control
of the trade union. The most progressive trade union leaders, opposing the pro-government CTC position, decided to take to the
streets and take over city halls. Fifty-five transportation workers occupied the Santiago de Cuba city hall for forty days. In the end,
they were ousted by the police and sent to local prisons.

Similar events took place in the western provinces. More than
400 cigar workers of the Cuban Land Tobacco Company occupied
the meeting hall of Santiago de Las Vegas to protest the closing of
their factory. In Colón the workers of the Zorrilla sugar mill seized the
city hall of Los Arabos when employers failed to start the harvest.[24]

As the practice of armed struggle evolved, the insurgent vanguard of the workers' movement matured, the leadership gradually
becoming aware that the key to the resolution of socioeconomic
conflict was the seizure of political power. As the workers' structures within the MR 26-7 were organized, the movement was able

to assume the role of a class, a development unprecedented in the practice of all other political parties.

The leaders of the workers' sections, operating as a cell network inside the structures of the CTC, went beyond economic demands and assumed a position of political opposition. First operating underground as part of the MR 26-7, a revolutionary CTC emerged to support the rebel army government in arms, providing advice on sabotage, propaganda, and finances. This vanguard was able to join the insurrectional struggle as had sugar, textile, henequen, electrical, telephone, and telegraph workers, organizing actions and strikes. Among the most prominent leaders were Edilio Díaz Crespo in the Zorrilla sugar mill; Eugenio Cabrera in the sugar region of Colón; Julián Alemán, secretary-general of the FPTT; and the Gil Perdomo brothers, electric and telephone workers from the Auténticos who constantly sabotaged power lines throughout the province. Their actions did not go unnoticed by the Matanzas government, especially in Colón, home of plantation owner Colonel Pedraza.

Workers' attacks against municipal halls occurred as the pro-amnesty movement for political prisoners developed, which originally intended to exclude the assailants of the Moncada. During the mobilizations, the outstanding labor leader of the Zorrilla sugar mill, Edilio Díaz Crespo, was hunted down and arrested by the army between Corralillo and Matanzas. Díaz Crespo had previously been accused of supporting rebellion and conspiring against the state.

In June the minister of the interior banned the Havana daily newspaper *La Calle,* published by Ortodoxo leader Luis Orlando Rodríguez. Several days later the government rejected his request to reopen his newspaper office. Fidel Castro noted that circumstances were propitious for launching a political-ideological campaign on behalf of the MR 26-7. By collecting funds to support the newspaper, MR 26-7 would demonstrate that it was impossible to oppose the regime through parliamentarian and electoral methods, implying that the only possible option for the opposition was armed insurgency. At the same time, FEU and the university council issued a public protest against the search conducted by the police at the University of Havana under the pretext of tips concerning hidden arms located on campus. Colonel Conrado Carratalá disclosed to the media that he had been informed of a "broad terrorist plan" led from Miami by Carlos Prío aimed at promoting a revolution in Cuba to overthrow the regime. Among the people involved, he claimed, were several university leaders.[25]

Prior to these events, however, the Batista government, in consultation with U.S. military officials, had decided to establish the Bureau to Repress Communist Activities in Cuba (Buró de Represión a las Actividades Comunistas; BRAC). Using this agency as a front, the regime disguised its true repressive objectives, aimed not so much against the Popular Socialist Party (Partido Socialista Popular; PSP), which in fact favored an electoral resolution of the crisis and thus was not a real threat to the regime, but against the development of a broader anti-Batista nationalist movement.

At any given moment of crisis since World War II, nationalist, democratic, liberal, and revolutionary forces had demonstrated their ability to join together around a left-wing program to oppose a repressive regime. The regime thus decided to intensify its repression of the revolutionary movement, including workers and students, during the summer of 1955 and indiscriminately accused organizations like the MR 26-7, the DR, the Auténtico Party Organization (Organización Auténtico; OA), and the AAA, whose methods and strategies were unrelated to and different from those of the PSP.

In statements made to a special correspondent of the *New York World Telegram* in July, Batista vowed to impede the return of communist political exiles.[26] He was, in fact, afraid that another insurrection would gain strength and he would be unable to crush it before the end of his term. Because the Eisenhower administration wanted to prevent the rise of a government of the revolutionary left, Batista's strategy was constantly and falsely to accuse the revolutionary nationalist movement of being communist.

* * *

By the end of 1953, the Batista government faced a deficit of $32 million and borrowed money from Cuba's National Bank. By the end of 1954, the accumulated deficit reached $665 million, the crisis having worsened because of two main factors: The government insisted upon maintaining a high level of expenditures against a decreasing income level and thus was forced to seek new sources of funds; and having depleted the legal capacity of direct loans from the National Bank, the government resorted to issuing public bonds to meet the treasury's obligations.

The initial 1954–1955 budgets were $18 million less than previous budgets, although the regime faced extra expenditures because of the November 1954 elections. To counter the shortfall in revenues, the government laid off public servants and cut wages and credit.[27] North American investments in Cuba increased all through 1955. The United States, for example, invested $43 million in the Nicaro nickel plant. In June the government of Cuba received a U.S. military mission led by Major General Robert W. Douglas and expanded the military assistance treaty between the two countries.[28]

In the course of these years, the popular movement varied only in form. From the beginning, students took direct part in the political struggle against Batista's regime through strikes, demonstrations, marches, and street actions. Workers at large engaged in the struggle on an economic level, trying to solve wage conflicts and unemployment through different kinds of strikes. In 1953 the confrontations increasingly became socioeconomic conflicts as the middle class and students took up the workers' plight. These gradually turned into antigovernment protests as the army intervened on behalf of employers. As the armed forces started repressing the trade union movement and supporting employers, the confrontation between capital and labor became a political-military conflict. Workers became aware that their interests were affected not only by employers but by armed forces, who used violence and harassment and jailed their top leaders. These circumstances convinced many of the need to join the armed struggle.

Differences between workers' interests and those of the progovernment CTC leaders sharpened as CTC leader Mujal remained aligned with the regime. The opposition in federations and trade unions became aware of the need to rally around a counterpart to the trade union movement to defend their interests against employers, the armed forces, and the policy of Mujal's CTC.

This need to join an insurrectional labor organization parallel to the CTC to defend the interests of workers against employers and the armed forces became most apparent in 1955. After June all groups started organizing around the workers' section and the National Workers' Front (Frente Obrero Nacional; FON) in factories, plantations, and other workplaces. The main feature of the insurrectional workers' movement was that its grassroot cells operated parallel to the trade union, often with active trade union leaders in top positions in the provincial federations and some even participating in the national CTC leadership or acting as members of employers' or government structures, as was the case of Auténtico member Conrado Bécquer, a sugar workers' leader who served in the Cuban legislature.

The MR 26-7 provincial and national workers' coordinators originated from trade unions representing the railroad, sugar, textile, rayon, liquor and beverage, and hotel and restaurant workers. Julián Alemán from Matanzas played an important role first as coordinator in his province and later in Havana and Pinar del Río. He was murdered by the regime in an underground action in 1958. Initially, he was replaced in Matanzas by Joaquín Torres, head of La Rayonera workers and later by Eugenio Cabrera, trade union leader of sugar workers in Colón.

The insurrectional tendency of the textile and sisal workers' sector was most pronounced at La Rayonera, La Jarcía, and the sisal plantations of Coliseo, Cárdenas, and Camarioca. In the sugar sector, Jaime López of the Dolores sugar mill and provincial workers leader of the Cuban People's Party (Orthodox) (Partido del Pueblo Cubano [Ortodoxo]; PPC[O]) in the FNTA, together with many trade union leaders of this sector in the regions of Colón, Cárdenas, Jovellanos, and Unión de Reyes, also joined the leadership of the workers' section and FON and subsequently took other positions in provincial workers' coordination bodies or became leaders of guerrilla detachments and heads of action and sabotage in Colón, Cárdenas, Coliseo, Agramonte, and Jagüey Grande. Many, such as Luis Crespo and Horacio Rodríguez, were sent by the provincial leaders of the MR 26-7 to Mexico to join the *Granma* expedition.

The potential for worker insurgency existed as of the morning of March 10, 1952, when a general political strike against the regime was set into motion almost spontaneously. Workers' insurgency began to take shape as labor elements and groups realized that their problems could not be solved through government mediation, because in its collaboration with employers, the regime used the armed forces to protect sugar mills, watch over the roads, and control labor conflicts by repressing the workers. The most experienced core of MR 26-7 leaders realized that labor militancy, expressed most dramatically through strikes, was developing among all worker sectors of the nation and understood the importance of this method in supporting insurrection against the regime.[29]

* * *

The strike movement that developed in the western provinces under the guidance of Auténtico trade union leader Pascasio Lineras, secretary-general of the FNTT, was supported in Matanzas

Province by Ortodoxo Julián Alemán, who organized the anti-Batista trade union movement.

Many leaders of trade locals as well as textile and sisal workers in the western provinces maintained their anti-Batista positions throughout the 1950s. In late 1952, sisal workers of the Arigüanabo textile plant had not yet received overdue payments. Workers of the Camarioca, Cárdenas, and Carbonera plantations in Matanzas had similarly gone unpaid. By the end of September, the Matanzas La Rayonera trade union began a work slowdown when Burke Hedges, owner of the company as well as a representative of the National Industrialists' Association (Asociación Nacional de Industriales) and personal friend of Fulgencio Batista, refused to provide a list of workers to permit the union to start labor negotiations. In late September the strike had reached the Arigüanabo textile plant, the Cubana Cordage in Güanajay, and La Jarcia in Matanzas. The Calabazar plants ceased operations, and the strike affected all clothing departments of Havana's largest stores.

The FNTT claimed that the stoppage involved some 30,000 workers. By early October more than 300 workers and trade union leaders in Havana were arrested and taken to the Castillo del Príncipe prison. More than 2,500 workers across the provinces were arrested by the rural guard.

A conciliatory meeting took place in Havana. Hedges of La Rayonera was among those who represented the industrialists; workers' representatives included Pascasio Lineras, secretary-general of the FNTT. A conflict erupted among industrialists when Hedges insisted that the problem was the result of a poorly conceived application of Decree 2144, which provided tax exemptions to rayon textile plants, and that if the exemptions were maintained, companies would be forced to close. For his part, Martín de Nicolás argued that domestic fibers had to be mixed with imported fibers. The debate revealed important differences among the industrialists.[30] Shortly thereafter, 160 sisal office and plantation workers of La Jarcia were arrested and charged with illegal assembly in the offices of the sisal workers' trade union in Cárdenas, where they had gathered to discuss the problems that had arisen with employers.

Between May 1953 and June 1954, La Rayonera workers began strike activities anew. They issued a manifesto to local authorities, the Ministry of Labor, and other national agencies requesting conciliatory arrangements in Decree 2144 to allow the importation of European-made fibers into the country. They maintained that this

measure would avoid worker layoffs and the attending conse-
quences of hunger and poverty.

The conflict persisted unresolved into September. Work slowdowns continued. Another meeting was held in November, attended by leaders of La Rayonera's workers' trade union and Mujal
of the CTC and Alemán of the FPTT. The workers of La Jarcia
plant and of sisal plantations complained to the minister of labor
that the company was obstructing the solution to the labor problem. The company, for its part, refused to accept any other solution
than plantation workers' wage cuts. In early 1954 the FNTT vowed
to stop all plantation and workshop operations if the demands of
the agricultural sisal sector were not met. In Matanzas the Yumurí
and Larrauri plantations and Las Carboneras in Cárdenas stopped
working.

The threats to lay off rayon workers and to reduce the wages of
textile and sisal workers resulted in a work stoppage. In January the
FNTT planned a ten-minute stoppage, including all sisal plantation
workers and those of La Rayonera, La Jarcia, and garment factories. The plan was to intensify the stoppage and gradually move toward a general strike. Further negotiations postponed the action.[31]

In February 1954 the situation took a turn for the worse. The
sector's mobilization expanded throughout the province. Alemán
skillfully handled the issue. As a result of the sisal workers' plenary,
the textile federation agreed that a committee led by Joaquín
Cotera, secretary-general of the CTC delegation, and made up of
delegates from all trade unions of the sector affected by the situation would meet with Mujal and Minister of Finances Gustavo
Gutiérrez. The plenary also agreed to mobilize all workers of
Matanzas Province and use billboards, manifestos, workers' rallies,
and meetings to inform the public of living conditions of the sisal
workers.

The FPTT delegation convened an executive committee meeting in the CTC's headquarters with the strikers to propose the
adoption of solidarity agreements with the strikers. Alemán and the
provincial executive decided that the stoppage inaugurated in May
1954 on the fourteen sisal plantations in support of the protest
movement should expand to Matanzas La Rayonera and other
plants of the sector. La Rayonera's stoppage would be gradual: one
hour the first day, to be extended daily until demands were met.
The sector's movement involved the industrialists' lack of compliance with Decree 848 of May 1953, declaring that rayon workers
were to collect 3 percent of the profits on fiber sold since May 1953

in order to subsidize workers laid off because of wage cuts. The enterprises owed $260,000 to this compensation fund.

Havana's Arigüanabo plant, owned by Burke Hedges, began its stoppage in the first week of May in solidarity with the movement that began at La Jarcia in Matanzas. It was led by Ortodoxo trade union leaders who also backed the insurgency movement against Batista. Thousands of workers left Havana's workshops before the arrival of army units. Similar events occurred in Cárdenas, Matanzas, San José de las Lajas, Cotorro, Guanabacoa, and other textile plants, where many workers were arrested.[32]

Conflicts and police actions increased in May. The textile strike worsened in Cárdenas and Camarioca, threatening to become indefinite. Once again employers asked for military intervention, expecting the Ministry of Labor to deal with the problem and support them. But the government had no more control over the sisal sector than did the employers. On this occasion, it was the sisal workers who declared the strike in support of the textile sector, expanding it to the plantations of the International Harvester Sisal Company near Varadero. Ortodoxo trade union leaders continued to attack the system in the western provinces by extending the protest movement to other plants and plantations of Matanzas and Havana. Juan Manuel Castellanos and other officers of La Estrella Agricultural Company were arrested. The secretary-general of the Fibers and Jarcia Industry at the San Antonio farm, accused of illegal assembly, was released by mid-May.[33]

The conflict was resolved at the same time. The federation gave the order to suspend the work stoppage, and the government released all workers arrested in Havana and Matanzas. The key to the success of the strike movement in Matanzas sisal plantations was that the federation expanded the confrontation through gradual stoppages in the textile and garments workshops of the Arigüanabo, La Rayonera, and other plants throughout the country. This measured strike was assuming general strike dimensions that would have closed the industry down.

Alemán's capabilities and skills were unquestionable. The minister of finance was forced to order sisal enterprises to pay the three cents per pound on fiber sold since May 1953 to compensate laid-off workers.[34]

But the government also introduced a military mechanism. A week after the end of the strike, the army charged textile and sisal workers' leaders with an illegal strike. First on the list of those arrested was Alemán.

Military action underlined the government's hostility toward the workers. In June 1954 the management of La Rayonera informed union delegate José Vega that a report for his dismissal was being filed. The temporary calm was broken. Protests began again, and army and rural guard agents "maintained tranquility in the workplace."[35]

In late June the executive committee of the rayon workers' trade union publicly denounced these actions. It also informed authorities that one of the spinners had suffered an embolism after being abused by members of the industrial supervision. The trade union charged that the company was transforming the plant into a concentration camp where workers were provoked so that the armed forces would intervene in the conflicts.

Relations between workers and La Rayonera were once again tense. The minister of labor issued a resolution ordering a three-day investigation into work conditions, the industry's cost-effectiveness, and workers' performances. Lemus Calderín, president of the workers' federation, had broken relations with the employers. For its part, the enterprise argued that the problem originated in a lack of discipline among workers, workers' threats, and the slow-down process that resulted in loss of output. A Rayonera workers' commission also informed the press that the enterprise planned to charge workers with sabotage.

The regime's repressive actions against workers and their trade union leaders in 1954 were not limited to the sugar, sisal, and textile sectors. Military actions were also taken against trade union leaders and workers of the Jovellanos Gravi sisal plant. One of the people arrested was trade union leader Gastón Martínez Planos, who was taken to the municipal prison and charged with inducing a strike in the industry.[36]

Trade union leaders and a large number of workers at the Betroma textile plant had started joining the MR 26-7 workers' cells. In July 1955 a group of workers exerted pressure on supervisors to leave their posts. Within a few days, they began the strike, were charged in the courts, and were subsequently imprisoned for two months. The economic situation of the relatives of the imprisoned workers was extremely difficult. Many of them organized a public fund-raising effort, asking drivers along the Vía Blanca highway, in front of Las Carboneras sisal plantations of Camarioca, to contribute to the cause. This action resulted in the arrest of Auténtico labor leaders Pascasio Lineras, secretary-general of the FNTT; Marcos Hernández, trade union leader of the plantation; and others.

The commander of the Matanzas Plácido Regiment, Colonel Pilar García, promised sisal workers a solution to the problems they had included in a list of demands by discussing them with the owner of the Larrauri Carboneras plantations. But the employers refused to agree with the workers on two additional *caballerías* (1 *caballeria* = 33.3 acres) to be planted with sisal and several provisions on wages.

At that time Alemán and other leaders of federations and trade unions had already joined the MR 26-7. The workers of the Jovellanos cordage company started protesting in mid-July 1955 against the low wages they were paid at Carboneras. Through their trade union's general-secretary, Marcos Hernández, they demanded wages for the period of forced time off they were obliged to take when the company closed down. Hernández reported that after discussing the preparation of new *caballerías* with the employers, they had not reached agreement concerning the "hunger wages." For its part, the company argued that it shut down the plant because of the high price of fiber, which made it impossible to continue production; it had asked the workers for a temporary suspension of the production of rope until the issue of the price was solved. Workers accepted this answer but were deceived: The company set up a new enterprise, violating the collective and seniority agreements with the trade union. La Jarcia plant in Matanzas where Alemán worked closed in August 1955. Employers had violated the wage freeze provision, and sisal workers renewed their protests under the insurgent leadership.[37] Thus began a period of direct action. In autumn 1955, sisal workers of Las Carboneras plantations in Cárdenas spontaneously launched sabotage actions.

La Jarcia workers took over the plant and were ousted by the army. Their leaders were arrested. In the Vía Blanca highway section between Matanzas and Varadero, in front of Las Carboneras, workers spread hooked nails, causing flat tires among passing cars. The Ministry of Labor attempted to solve the conflict at La Jarcia by making employers and workers commit themselves to reduce production costs and avoid the closing of the industry.[38]

Three hundred workers were laid off during the month of October. Others were subject to wage cuts at Rayonera Cubana. The regime took over the industry militarily, and three workers were accused of sabotage. The enterprise announced the plant's closing in mid-October. The workers at La Jarcia agreed to shut down their plant as a gesture of public support for La Rayonera workers.

The trade union asked for and received permission from the provincial labor office to meet at the FPTT offices and the offices of the provincial CTC. They met and were rousted by the armed forces that night. The workers then decided to launch a protest movement that very day with a work slowdown in all departments of La Rayonera to oppose potential layoffs. They considered the option of a general strike if no agreement were reached.

Workers of the Química-Comercial and Fomentos Químicos plants, affiliated with La Rayonera, left their jobs in late October as they had been instructed by trade union delegate Agapito Gil Placencia. They also stopped the carbon bisulfate plant; the sulfuric acid plant continued operating provisionally, under the responsibility of the company's supervisors.

In November the Ministry of the Interior instituted measures against workers' assemblies. This provoked the protest of rayon workers, whose scheduled assembly had been suspended. Workers previously laid off from the Yumurí henequen company demanded work and the reopening of the sisal plantations that had been idle for more than a year. Rayon workers continued to organize protest meetings in December, the immediate provocation being the enterprise's refusal to make advanced payments, as was traditionally done for Christmas, and to grant vacations and paid sick leave.[39]

The workers of La Jarcia, led by Alemán (by then engaged fully in insurgent underground activities), once again initiated a work slowdown and finally left their jobs in support of the sugar workers' general strike of December 1955. La Jarcia filed against the workers in the courts and threatened that if workers did not return to their jobs, management would dismiss them.[40]

In January 1956 La Rayonera workers complained about the pressures exerted by their bosses and called upon their union leaders to take measures. They also complained that the enterprise, in laying off worker Pedro Torres, had precipitated the layoffs of thousands of workers who were going to be "thrown into lives of hunger and poverty." The FNTT's provincial and national leadership supported the rayon workers' movement. At the special session that took place in Matanzas, they claimed that if the treaty were put into effect, "it would mean havoc for thousands of workers."[41]

In early 1957, many of these workers, too, became active participants in the developing insurgency in the province. The center of MR 26-7's conspiratorial activities in Matanzas—in preparation for the general insurrection—was in the offices of the headquarters of the FPTT and the provincial CTC. Aldo Santamaría, provincial chief of the MR 26-7 between 1955 and late 1956, used the location as his headquarters, and the underground provincial leadership operated from there through the end of 1956. Joaquín Torres, who had joined the MR 26-7's workers' section and was later appointed workers' provincial coordinator, stood out among La Rayonera fighters. The regime charged him with receiving and distributing the Fidelista underground newspaper *Revolución* and sending 5,000 copies to Matanzas. Journalist Carlos Franqui confessed to being the editor of the bulletin.

By early 1957 La Jarcia had separated from the agricultural sector and was receiving sisal from other plantations.[42] Several months later the employers decided to close the Betroma textile plant permanently, arguing that they had not received the subsidy to which they were entitled to compensate for foreign competition. The provincial CTC was seeking to avoid the shutdown, which would affect some 250 families in Matanzas. The middle classes and civic institutions protested the situation, the Rotary and Lions Clubs declaring their support for the workers.[43]

In January 1958 La Rayonera management proposed to increase production to compete with foreign companies. This meant that 200 workers were to be released. A few weeks later the company imposed a job rotation system in the plant that signified a 16 percent wage cut. The workers considered the action unfair, since prices of all consumer commodities had risen tremendously during the first quarter of 1958.[44] Workers met with the trade union, which agreed to mobilize its forces and organize a written press and radio campaign to inform the authorities about a planned layoff. They also requested the Ministry of Labor to deal with the matter.

Another conflict arose in spring 1958 at Camarioca, where several problems such as row planting, work stoppages, and advanced payments at La Conchita sisal plantations were under discussion. At a meeting at the Ministry of Labor, the enterprise announced a production stoppage for three months. The trade union leadership complained that the stoppage would coincide with preparations for the April 9 strike of the MR 26-7's provincial workers' section led by Quino Torres. In April employers refused to give La Conchita plantations' sisal workers advanced payments. The trade union denounced these irregularities before the Ministry of Labor but was ignored.

Several weeks later, after ninety days of inactivity, La Estrella sisal company of Cárdenas tried to start operations by laying off twenty-two workers and transferring forty-five to other, lower-paying jobs. The CTC said this would not be allowed and demanded that the enterprise resume operations with all the staff in their previous positions. Some 300 sisal workers had been affected by the refusal to advance payments.[45]

The situation worsened when La Conchita started fumigating sisal plantations by air. The insecticide destroyed the small crops that peasants used to feed their families. When La Conchita workers protested and requested the company to go back to a manual fumigation system, employers refused and took repressive measures. This motivated the workers in preparing for the general political strike and supporting armed actions in the territory.

* * *

In July 1953, only weeks before the attack on the Moncada and Bayamo garrisons, trolley cars in Matanzas halted operations when the company was unable to pay its $22,000 debt to the Cuban Electric Company. Members of the Labor Commission went to Havana to negotiate a possible incorporation of trolley car workers into local bus enterprises. Trolley car workers threatened to take over the Matanzas city hall if no solution were found. Protests continued. By mid-July, since workers were not receiving their wages, they also demanded payment for vacation time. Despite all efforts, the demands were not met, and the trolley car company was accused of negligence.[46]

From 1953 to 1954, worker-management confrontations intensified in the ports of Matanzas and Cárdenas. The National Maritime Workers' Federation (Federación Obrera Marítima Nacional; FOMN) intervened in the conflict on June 1954 to organize a general assembly of the workers and to reorganize the sector's trade union from top to bottom.

The process of purging port workers' leaders who attacked the FOMN continued. The workers complained that the foreman was not using the work rotation list and that the trade union delegate was not doing his duty of appointing stevedores and guaranteeing enforcement of the list. Several months later, part-time workers of the port guild condemned their employers for refusing to pay their vacations, as previously agreed upon. In Cárdenas the police suspended the port workers' trade union assembly, scheduled to hold elections.[47]

In early 1954 the Matanzas cigar workers' union supported a strike of the Havana cigar workers against subsidy cuts. As the situation worsened, Batista was forced to intervene. The workers accepted an end to the stoppage once the president of the republic and the CTC promised to meet their demands.[48]

By 1955 the crisis reached shoemakers, who denounced whole-salers and declared a production stoppage. In August the Yumurí tire plant imposed wage cuts and increases in minimal levels of pro-duction to reinitiate work; workers refused to accept these actions, and accordingly the leaders of one of the trade unions were charged with illicit strike a few weeks later. Colonel Pilar García called the leadership of the plant's trade union to a meeting in mid-October at the Goicuría Garrison and committed himself to taking urgent measures to solve the worker-employer problem. Two weeks later, relations between workers and employers shattered. The sec-retary-general of the national federation of workers in the chemi-cal industry said that the workers of the Yumurí tire plant were maintaining "their struggle and demands against the enterprise," which had declared a lockout and closed the plant, leaving more than 300 workers without jobs.[49]

Toward the end of October 1955, the police attacked the par-ticipants in rallies held at the Libertad Park in Matanzas. The fol-lowing morning the president of the court of justice and the chief district attorney met to determine responsibilities incurred by gov-ernment agents.

At the same time, the buses of urban enterprises operated under army and police supervision to prevent stoppages. Gas sta-tions started running short of gas. Union members did not report to work at the Sauto Theater. The retailers' union guaranteed the dis-tribution of some commodities, beers, and sodas. The graphic arts trade union agreed to stop work.[50]

In the midst of the social upheaval that deepened during the second half of 1955, telegraph workers also organized a strike. Par-ticipation of civil servants was massive, and many were arrested to-gether with their trade union leaders. More than 200 messengers and telegraph workers of the Ministry of Communications who joined the strike were threatened with dismissals and layoffs. Many mail and telegraph workers' leaders and employees subsequently joined the insurrectional struggle against the regime through the MR 26-7.[51]

The activity of Cuban Electric Company workers in sabotage actions and strikes since March 1952 was so great that by 1957 Batista authorized the replacement of the employees. In May 1957 an official commission of Matanzas made up of company execu-tives hired new employees to protect the company from strikers, thereby worsening the situation and intensifying electrical workers' protests.

Many company workers were arrested and charged with sabotage as electric, telegraph, and telephone lines were broken and transformers and posts destroyed, particularly in the municipalities of Los Arabos, Perico, Colón, Cárdenas, and Matanzas.

Another important strike took place in August 1955 involving the bank workers trade union. The pro-government CTC issued a document signed by its secretary-general condemning the work slowdown and "idle arms" strike announced by union leaders. By the second week of September, Batista and Cardinal Arteaga intervened. Some leaders of the strike were also chiefs of the MR 26-7 workers' movement, including the provincial bank workers' secretary, José María de la Aguilera, and trade union leader Enrique Hart. Hart would later move to Matanzas to become one of the main leaders of the underground and the MR 26-7 military structure in the province.[52]

Other worker sectors joined the protest movement in early 1958. The workers of Canteras and the Matanzas gypsum and brick plants remained jobless. Provincial CTC leader Joaquín Cotera requested a meeting with military chief Pilar García to discuss the issue in January. Meanwhile, employees of clinics and laboratories joined the national campaign in favor of a 20 percent wage increase.[53]

In essence, the problem was a manipulation of the workers' sector by the state and employers, using leaders of the pro-government CTC, the army, and the police. The Gordian knot created by the political system could be cut only by an insurgent workers' movement—specifically, by a general political strike to support the insurrection against a regime that maintained and defended interests contrary to workers' needs.

After the failure of the April 9, 1958, strike, the provincial MR 26-7 leadership began to organize groups of rebels into armed detachments. The military chiefs of the Mario Muñoz Detachment and the René Fraga Moreno Unit were sugar workers' trade union leaders. An electrical worker led the Enrique Hart Detachment. By the end of 1958, all were operating in the regions of Cárdenas and Colón. Although the party had previously been opposed to armed struggle, PSP guerrilla groups were organized during the last week of December 1958. They were led by two workers of the sugar agroindustrial sector.

* * *

The sugar industry, the main economic pillar of the republic, was the sector most protected by the regime and, in return, most pro-government. Labor conflicts between plantation owners and industrial workers and between farmers and agricultural workers were not resolved between 1952 and 1958. One of the most important strikes of 1955 was that of the sugar workers, led by the FNTA with the support of the FEU. Conrado Rodríguez and Conrado Bécquer, the key leaders of the FNTA, and José Antonio Echeverría, Fructuoso Rodríguez, and other FEU leaders played prominent roles in the conflict, which began with the demand for the sugar bonus payment but evolved into a general political strike.

The first trials of peasants arrested by the army and charged with burning sugarcane fields in Carlos Rojas, Jovellanos, Pedro Betancourt, and Alacranes were held in January 1953.[54] Between July 30 and August 10, several sabotage actions were carried out by the industrial workers of the Arrechabala refinery of Cárdenas, where a fire destroyed two warehouses.[55] A strong insurrectional movement had developed in this plant in the 1930s, its workers pioneering the organization of trade unions in the province. By mid-October 1953, plantation owners delayed repairs in several sugar mills of the province, including the Mercedes, Alava, Por Fuerza, and Conchita mills as a means to cut workers' wages.[56]

The army provided protection for all sugar mills and plantations to prevent acts of arson. The provincial press praised the work done by army officer Pérez Coujil in "resolving the problem that had come up among workers, farmers, and plantation owners." Conflicts had apparently ended in most sugar mills and plantations during the first quarter of 1954, except for the mills of Puerto and Limones that had not yet started their milling season.[57]

The socioeconomic struggles of the townships of Guamacaro and Limonar signaled a period of uninterrupted conflict among workers, employers, the armed forces, and the government in this section of the province. In other regions, including Colón, Cárdenas, Jovellanos, and Unión de Reyes, a powerful group of sugar workers' trade union leaders stood out. Such was the case of the Zorrilla sugar mill trade union in Colón, which since 1953 had confronted all political-military actions and decided to take over city hall if their demands were not met. In December 1953 the Zorrilla workers held an assembly with the participation of trade union leaders from different areas of the province of Matanzas and delegates from the sector's trade unions. The objective of all those groups was to support the FNTA in any statement it made concerning the coming harvest. Among those in attendance was the outstanding Ortodoxo grassroots fighter Edilio Díaz Crespo, who since the March 10 coup had advocated insurrection. Also present was an Ortodoxo leader of the sugar regional of Colón, Eugenio Cabrera.[58]

In February 1954 the workers of Limones requested that the sugar mill be turned over to the state or to the workers to resolve the labor problem caused when the company fired 128 workers. The conflict reached Batista. Since 1954 the working classes of the *batey* (mill town) and township of Limones had demanded the intervention of the mayor due to the local economic hardships. The conflict not only delayed the start of the harvest but left more than 100 families of the area in extreme poverty. For their part, the *colonos* demanded the transfer of their quota to other sugar mills.

The Ministry of Labor solved the problem together with the employers by reinstating the 128 workers. But by the end of the year, as repairs were to begin, the mill once again took restrictive economic measures, resulting in the workers' mobilization. This affected the Puerto and Zorrilla mills as well.

The working class of the area once again mobilized in November 1954 in response to the terrible economic impact of the conflict. Trade union leaders together with local citizens decided to try to stop the *colonos* from taking their sugar cane to other sugar mills.[59]

With the beginning of the Limones conflict, the sugarcane plantations of nearby municipalities became more vulnerable to arson attacks. In Bolondrón and Pedro Betancourt, fire destroyed 200,000 *arrobas* (1 *arroba* = 25 lbs.) of cane and extended to potato warehouses and other facilities.[60]

In the Cuba mill, trade union leaders ordered a work stoppage until *colonos* paid wages owed to the agricultural workers. Domingo Casanova Orihuela, secretary of the mill trade union, and Reynaldo Domínguez, provincial leader of the FNTA, were arrested. The sugar mill's manager said that there were some half million *arrobas* of cane in the *batey* that could not be milled.[61]

Meanwhile, sabotage continued. Several fields were torched in January and February 1954 in Colón and Alacranes. Other large fields were burned in the Susana and Deseada farms of the Tinguaro sugar mill, and the workers of La Conchita sugar mill protested against the threats and harassment of the Alacranes rural guard, which charged workers for burning the mill's cane fields. Workers of the Zorrilla sugar mill of Los Arabos refused to start the harvest in January, demanding the reinstatement of laid-off workers. The conflict continued until March with *colonos* arguing that the company that owned the sugar mill would not pay off its debts.

During this period, telephone and telegraph workers sabotaged lines near the city of Colón.

A conflict similar to that of the Limones mill came up in Jagüey Grande's Australia mill. The *batey* and Jagüey's populations were mobilized to support workers' protests after a large group of workers were laid off, and the railroad's sidetrack was sabotaged.[62] In July the workers insisted that the mill resolve its differences with the mill's retail department and pay advances to workers during the idle season on the basis of the coming harvest. If the request was not met, they recommended that the FNTA arrange a $50,000 bank credit to mitigate the workers' economic hardships. In October the administration reported that repairs would begin in the mills for a minimum of thirty-five to forty days and that they would use fewer workers. The trade union claimed that workers who complained about this measure were threatened with layoffs.[63]

The situation worsened in the Soledad mill of Jovellanos. The workers threatened to take over the sugar mill if work did not start as a result of differences between owners and farmers. The trade union leadership instructed a sector of workers to leave their jobs as a way to prevent those who remained from doing their tasks. Management denounced these partial strike tactics, and the army was ordered to investigate. Worker-employer confrontations also continued at the Limones mill, with the difference that the FNTA's provincial leadership announced a potential strike in all sugar mills of the province in support of workers' demands.[64]

Problems among the FNTA, plantation owners, and *colonos* peaked in December 1955. The FNTA's provincial executive agreed to declare a general strike in all industrial and agricultural activities of the twenty-four sugar mills of Matanzas if plantation owners did not pay the 1954 harvest sugar price difference before Christmas eve. A day later, all sugar mills and plantations were paralyzed; the mass arrest of workers and labor leaders followed. Plantation owners publicly stated that they were not in a position to pay wages that did not correspond to sugar prices.

The strike was supported by many sectors. In Unión de Reyes, workers of the Santo Domingo sugar mill walked off their jobs on December 29 following instructions of trade union secretary-general Digno Nicolás. The union members of the Perret Foundry also stopped working.[65]

In early 1956 the conflict that had provoked the sugar workers' general strike continued unresolved. In Colón, San José de los Ramos, Los Arabos, and Manguito, the sugar regional of the Alava,

Mercedes, Zorrilla, Araujo, and Por Fuerza sugar mills agreed in late January not to start the harvest of the mills in those jurisdictions until the price difference the farmers refused to comply with was paid to agricultural workers. The FNTA's regional leadership, aware that the conflict between the mill plantation owners and workers persisted, ratified its strategy of paralyzing all harvest activity until the problem was solved.

Industrial and agricultural workers at the Araujo mill, in accordance with instructions from the local trade unions of the CTC and the FNTA, did not return to the factory or sugarcane fields as a result of management's refusal to ratify the seniority system. The union denounced the mill and said that unless the problem was solved within one week, milling would not begin. By February the conflict was resolved and workers returned to the mill.

In May 1956, when discussions began in the Zorrilla mill, the company's refusal to pay surplus production, in violation of the law, caused widespread indignation among workers. The protest by workers worsened to such an extent that many feared serious disorder, whereupon the minister of labor intervened. The burning of sugarcane fields had begun once again; in the fields of the Yaguasa farm of the Murga Sibu neighborhood, 30,000 *arrobas* were burned.[66]

By mid-1956 in the Santa Rita mill, a clash ensued when the *colonos* refused to pay holidays. In the Araujo and Alava sugar mills, problems arose when employers wanted to pay a salary of only sixty to eighty cents a day. Agricultural workers also claimed that local food stores were engaged in a price-fixing scheme, resulting in a 40 percent increase in the prices of basic commodities.[67]

Workers of the Limones mill organized a rally in June 1956 in Limonar to protest against the mill's refusal to pay surplus production. They denounced irregularities in the enterprise, especially by the manager of the industry. Several weeks later they resisted management's attempt to increase the mill's profits by violating the law and expanding into two work shifts for fixed personnel while others were without work.[68]

A conciliatory board made up of representatives of labor and management met during the summer to discuss the variety of problems at the Australia mill in Jagüey. One was the conflict triggered when the mill began dismissal proceedings against stevedores. Another involved management's cancellation of train service from Ciénaga de Zapata to the Bahía de Cochinos, which would leave many workers stranded from their jobs.[69]

In July and September, Tinguaros workers were charged with declaring an illegal strike by refusing to load sugar bound for the United States to protest nonpayment of the sugar price difference bonus.[70]

Irregularities in pro-government trade union elections in August 1956 provoked a crisis within the FNTA. At elections at the Por Fuerza mill, workers claimed that because not all of the 2,000 workers had received their voter registration forms, only 500 workers could vote. At the Arrechabala refinery in Cárdenas, workers argued that they were being forced to vote for the secretary-general and candidates backed by the employers; they demanded another candidate, backed by the majority of the industry's trade union members. At the Dolores mill, trade unions similarly protested the list of candidates, and the Tinguaro mill workers complained to the provincial labor office. Many workers of the Alava sugar mill questioned the process by which delegates were appointed to represent them at the national sugar workers' congress. The police attacked demonstrators and arrested trade union leaders of the Dolores sugar mill, charging them with "insulting the government" and "having an illegal radio program." One of the key figures in these actions was Ortodoxo trade union leader Jaime López, who the year before had been chief of the MR 26-7 in the province at the request of Fidel Castro.[71]

In Matanzas Province the Canimar company continued to take measures contrary to workers' interests in the Limones mill. Repairs and agreements with the trade unions were again the subject of conflict. Management refused to discuss with union leaders the problem of collective work contracts and compliance with a ministerial resolution ordering the beginning of repairs. Once again the trade union asked for government intervention in the sugar mill, since the other twenty-three sugar mills of the province had started the harvest. The FEU fully supported the demands of the workers and requested the mill to start repairs and apply the new wage increase. In October the workers announced they would hold a general assembly of the sugar mill workers.

In Zorrilla the workers refused to start repairs if their demands were not met; they went on strike and were arrested. The following month 5,000 *arrobas* of sugarcane were burned. The rural guard never discovered how the fire began.

In December sugar worker trade union leaders requested assistance regarding the problem of repairs in the Australia mill, which had finished repairs to roads, works, and wagons five days after they began, creating uneasiness among the workers.[72]

In late 1956 in Calimete, a group of peasant leaders of the trade union of La Vega farm in Manguito were accused of illegal strike and arrested by the rural guard. Other disturbances took place in the region. A labor inspector was appointed to the Mercedes mill in Calimete to investigate layoffs among agricultural workers after Víctor Pomares, secretary-general of the sugar mill's trade union, argued that the mill was not laying off workers according to seniority.[73]

In late 1956 and early 1957, the activities of student and worker commandos of the MR 26-7 expanded in all regions of Mantanzas. The MR 26-7 provincial and regional workers' coordinators intensified their work in preparation for the revolutionary general strike. In the trade union at the plants and plantations, militants acted within their cells and continued to confront the employers and the regime. The trade union executive of the Limones mill started the year 1957 by presenting a list of demands to the company. One was to take steps to collect a 6 percent wage during the "dead season" in compliance with the national agricultural agreement.

The economic conditions originally created in the Limones mill and others in the province sharpened social conflict in the local townships, leading to government intervention but only a partial solution to the conflict. Further tensions related to the layoff of hundreds of workers in the other twenty-three Matanzas sugar mills, who were paid either poverty salaries or were never paid for overproduction. The problems of slowdowns, layoffs, and nonpayment of surplus production reflected the problems of the society as a whole.

In a plenary session, the FNTA agreed to promote the creation of new industries to provide employment for sugar workers during the "dead season," to adopt drastic measures against the speculation, and to end the policy of workers' displacements by the Atlantic Gulf Company. Trade union leaders demanded that the Zorrilla, Dos Rosas, Puerto, and Elena sugar mills pay surplus production. They also agreed to request fair taxes of agricultural workers' wages and the construction of homes for poor peasants. The workers concluded the assembly by supporting the national integration rally scheduled for April in Matanzas.[74] In essence, the sugar sector's workers and leaders favored transformations leading to a revolutionary solution. The revolutionary germ grew within the trade union movement of the pro-government CTC.

The most significant sabotage in the province and in all the western part of the country was the burning of the Tinguaro sugar mill in May 1957, which cost the government $5 million. That same day there was a confrontation between the army and the MR 26-7 revolutionary workers in the *batey,* where a rural guard sergeant was wounded. Further sabotage occurred against the España Republicana mill and the Matanzas sugar refinery.

In response to this and other acts of sabotage, Colonel Pilar García ordered military chiefs of squadrons in Matanzas and Perico to investigate. In their report these chiefs said that the sabotage had been planned by the MR 26-7 leaders of the province as part of the "insurrectional movement led by Fidel Castro to overthrow the government." In pursuit of that purpose, the report specified that they had "organized the July 26 Movement into cells in the Perico district" and the Tinguaro sugar mill, whose cells had been "given different missions to keep that area active."[75]

The trade union of the Australia mill in Jagüey Grande questioned surplus production payments because the enterprise had not included the team of stevedores doing piecework. Meanwhile, the *colonos* tried to violate the minimal agricultural wage provision, for which they were denounced by the workers' leaders in the municipality of Jagüey. Atlantic Gulf, owner of the Alava mill in Colón, refused to pay surplus production. Once the sugar mill's trade union realized it was impossible to solve the issue, it gave orders to limit the personnel who dismantled the carts and other mill equipment, effectively threatening to paralyze sugar shipments.[76]

After the failed April 9 strike, the FNTA referred to the need of solving issues such as leasing, introducing electricity in the *batey,* making advance payments to industrial workers, and debts to the sugar workers' retirement fund at the Limones mill. Colonel Pedraza, owner of the Zorrilla mill, clashed with the FNTA, refusing to pay wages to workers for the period the plant had stopped because of rain. Workers also protested the deplorable conditions at the mill, on the *batey,* and in the fields.[77]

During the last quarter of 1958, MR 26-7's provincial leadership in Matanzas prepared for advancement into the western provinces. Meanwhile, the MR 26-7 workers' section and the FON readied their provincial labor representative for an insurgent assembly called in a zone controlled by guerrillas on the northern front of Las Villas.

Many participants and leaders of the MR 26-7's urban guerrilla resistance and in Matanzas emerged from the sugar, textile, and sisal agroindustrial sectors. Although students played a fundamental role during the early years of the period, after 1955 the working class became the basis of the insurgency in Matanzas.[78]

4

The July 26 Movement: Spontaneous Mobilization, Resistance, and Insurrection

To understand the spontaneous character of the mobilization against the government of Fulgencio Batista, the coup d'état, and the leading role that people from liberal sectors and professions played in the insurgency, one must take account of the ideals of purity, honesty, and national identity in the struggle for political and social justice. One representative of such values was physician Mario Muñoz, the first chief of the MR 26-7 in Matanzas Province. As a professional with far more modest social origins than others in the middle class, he was intransigent in his views and behavior concerning the political and bureaucratic corruption that had characterized so much of the republic's history.

Muñoz and other figures active in the 1930 revolutionary conflicts considered Batista the leader of a counterrevolution that curbed and frustrated the revolution of 1933. Batista's counterrevolution took place both on a national level, with the overthrow of the reformist government on January 14, 1934, and on a hemispheric level, with the proposals of the Cuban delegation to the Seventh Inter-American Conference in December 1933 concerning the recognition of national governments, which Batista made without consulting the United States, and the annulment of the Platt amendment.[1] Batista crushed the Cuban liberation movement in 1935 with the murder of Antonio Guiteras, leader of Young Cuba in Matanzas, as he was about to leave for Mexico to organize an expeditionary force to promote the people's armed uprising. He also split the revolutionary movement into followers and critics of Batista's legitimacy.

During the 1940s Muñoz was motivated by the so-called "Auténtico revolution," but he soon recognized its weaknesses. He resigned from his position as physician at the emergency center of Colón in 1946 because he opposed the local politicians who intended to use his political, revolutionary, and humanist prestige among the lower and middle classes to win votes for that year's partial elections. He further opposed the corrupt administration of Ramón Grau San Martín.

Muñoz met Fidel Castro during the Ortodoxo electoral campaign. In 1950 he joined the PPC(O), attracted by its political platform. After the death of Eduardo Chibás, he traveled to Havana to meet Fidel Castro. Upon returning to Colón, he concluded that Castro was the only man who could replace Chibás.

Like Chibás, Muñoz believed in national identity: in the patriotic struggle reflecting Martí's ideals and the integration of all social sectors and classes for the advancement of the Cuban nation and the country's economic independence, political liberty, and sovereignty. He believed in social justice and the elimination of economic inequalities between the poor and the rich. His actions against the Batista government in 1934; his participation in creating an insurrectional organization with the DEU, which included sabotage, agitation, and propaganda activities; as well as his work with the March 1935 strike provided him with the experience to undertake similar activities in 1952–1953 when the Moncada Project was being devised.

The reaction to Batista's coup d'état was immediate in the capital and in many provincial capital cities. In Matanzas and the smaller municipalities such as Cárdenas, Colón, Jovellanos, and Agramonte, different sectors of the population spontaneously gathered at student centers and workplaces and in parks and city halls, or converged upon army garrisons still under the control of pro-Prío commanders to seek weapons to defend democracy and the 1940 constitution. Muñoz went to the Colón city hall, where he stayed for hours among the crowds, as the most outspoken individuals denounced Batista and demanded weapons to resist the coup. The Auténtico mayor committed himself to request arms from the rural guard's garrison but never did so.

Several weeks later, Muñoz was appointed chief of the movement in Matanzas and member of its national leadership. His leadership role in the western zone provided the historical continuity of the revolutionary movement that in the 1930s both inherited the 1895 revolution and established the basis for the new political force that emerged in the 1950s. The Ortodoxo group intended to organize the structures created by Chibás to conclude the revolution by overthrowing Batista. The youth followed Muñoz because they saw in him a man of action. Because of his experience and prestige among his fellow citizens and his ideas and activities in defending justice, humanity, and progress, those who initiated the sabotage in March 1952 in Matanzas gathered under his leadership and joined the conspiracy promoted by the new generation of the centennial.[2]

A new political force initially known as "the movement"—the MR 26-7—emerged in 1953, with the development of the Moncada Project. From its outset, the organization did not intend to be independent but to become a contributing force in the effort to overthrow the Batista dictatorship, as part of the PPC(O), which (in line with Chibás's thinking) was to have been in the vanguard of the struggle against Batista.[3]

In the beginning organizers modeled their movement's structures on those of Chibás's network of supporters. They paid particular attention to the proposition of a united opposition, and some Auténtico and Ortodoxo elements began to allude to the need for armed struggle. The group decided upon a military strategy and started organizing the Ortodoxo masses. Besides the civilian structure, the leadership established and trained action groups.

Castro expanded the Moncada plan to take over the garrisons and initiate a revolutionary general strike. To do this, the movement would distribute weapons to the population, incite the province to uprise, and instigate a strike, based on the people's general opposition to the regime. In essence, it was the same methodology and strategy followed during the entire fighting process against the dictatorship: a combination of armed struggle and political general strike.[4]

Castro's initial plan in 1953 was to call for a political strike if the Moncada garrison were taken over. If this was not possible, and if the rebels failed to defend the city, they planned retreat to the Sierra Maestra. The Ortodoxo masses formed the foundation of the movement's action groups and cells, which expanded with the incorporation of other social groups and sectors, creating this revolutionary structure led by Castro and Abel Santamaría.

While national organizers were structuring the movement in Havana and Pinar del Río Provinces, Muñoz worked in Matanzas. Muñoz first met with Castro and Santamaría in Havana in May 1952. The three later met in Colón to confirm Muñoz's task in the preparations for the armed uprising: to set up a radio power plant for agitation and propaganda plans to supplement the role of the underground newspaper *El Acusador.* Muñoz created a set of cells in

the region of Colón, participated with the leaders of the FEU in organizing the May 1952 celebrations, and mobilized the people in
different municipalities to pledge allegiance to the constitution and
repudiate the March coup d'état.[5]

The movement's cells supported FEU and secondary school centers in municipalities and sugar mills where the PPC(O)'s network was
strong. Important confrontations occurred in the capital city of the
province, as well as Colón, Cárdenas, Jovellanos, Pedro Betancourt,
and Agramonte.

* * *

During the period 1952–1953, repression intensified and arrests
increased. The youth used Radio Matanzas in their antigovernment
campaign. On several occasions the police attacked speakers in
public, both at the radio station and on the street. Not only Ortodoxos and students were arrested, but in the town of Jagüey several
citizens and former police officers were arrested in mid-June for
conspiring against the regime. In Colón antielection leaflets appeared. Public rallies against the regime and protests against elections organized by the government were also held in the town of
Máximo Gómez.[6]

A student named Rubén Batista was wounded in January 1953
at a Havana demonstration in tribute to Julio Antonio Mella. Matanzas students organized several rallies condemning the regime; they
occupied the secondary education institute, the school of commerce,
and the teachers' training school. The head of the Matanzas teachers' training school, René Fraga Moreno, who had joined the insurgency at the beginning, was one of the principal participants.[7]

The members of the movement had been told to keep a low
profile during street actions, as utmost secrecy on military preparations had to be maintained. Zero hour was made public to the
members of the cells selected to participate in the attack against the
Moncada and Bayamo garrisons a few months later.

In mid-July 1953, on Muñoz's forty-first birthday, Castro met
up with Muñoz and others who were to take part in the Moncado
attack. Muñoz was one of the first to put on the rebels' olive green
uniform, but Castro convinced him to dress as a doctor, since he
was to join the group led by Santamaría in taking over the garrison's Saturnino Lora Hospital. Once they had control of the garrison, because of his skills in radio techniques, Muñoz was to guarantee the broadcast of Raúl Gómez García's harangue to the people

by reading the Moncada manifesto and playing a recording of Chibás's speech called "The Last Knock," which was to signal the Ortodoxo masses to mobilize.[8]

Muñoz's car was the last to leave Santiago de Cuba for Moncada. He was accompanied by Julio Reyes from Matanzas, Raúl Gómez García, Haydée Santamaría, and Melba Hernández. Under fire from the army, Muñoz drove to the entrance of the hospital, and he and his fellow rebels entered the hospital.

The hospital's vanguard fought from the rear windows of the building, in front of the Moncada garrison. Muñoz, worried about the prolonged shooting, searched for a possible exit to withdraw if necessary, but found none. The shooting outside had ceased when the rebels realized they had not won. Muñoz ripped his name tag from his pocket, but police and SIM agent Angel Esteban Garay, who had hidden in the ward during the attack, identified him when police and soldiers arrived at the building. Shortly thereafter, he was murdered.

The chief of the medical college of Santiago de Cuba requested the body, and it was delivered on July 27. Muñoz was buried at the Santiago de Cuba Santa Efigenia cemetery early the following morning. His death was made public in the Colón newspapers.[9]

* * *

According to court records for 1952–1958, the army charged members of opposition movements with possession of weapons and explosives, sabotage and bomb explosions, holding worker and student strikes and workers' demonstrations against the government, distributing subversive propaganda and leaflets, publishing misleading manifestos and articles against the government, and burning sugarcane fields.[10] In March 1952, before the movement was formally organized, sworn statements in the courts already reflected the result of these spontaneous methods of struggle. When it became the MR 26-7, the movement adopted these tactics as part of its broader strategy of overthrowing the regime and seizing political power.[11]

Between 1952 and 1953, the movement became the main vanguard of the insurgency, not only uniting different sectors of the antigovernment opposition but also backing Chibás's program incorporating the ideals of Martí and demanding honesty from public officials and obtaining weapons to distribute to the people. During 1954 and 1955, when the amnesty was issued, the cells of the movement continued to work, until it was reorganized under the name "Movimiento Revolucionario 26 de Julio."

The organization and the revolutionary project were adapted for three stages: the attack on the Moncada and Bayamo garrisons (1952–1953), the expeditionary landing and general uprising planned by the MR 26-7 throughout the island (1955–1956), and the war waged by the rebel army with a military structure and politico-civic-military leadership in all provinces and in exile in the United States, Latin America, and Europe (1957–1958).

Between 1953 and 1958, Castro realized that it was extremely important to organize a military apparatus to overthrow the government, not only with an urban organization but also through a guerrilla army that was to become an instrument of the people's struggle against Batista's army. This was one of the greatest merits of his leadership: his understanding of how to structure the forces of resistance in the civil and military sphere and interpret and use popular methods of struggle to confront the violence and terror that defined the Batista regime. In political terms, Castro simply recovered the popular basis of the Chibás program and different forms of grassroots action, adding to those an insurgent organization throughout the island and among Cuban expatriates as a source of support for the revolutionary project. From the very beginning, Castro waved the banners of liberty and the just republic envisioned by Martí.

In methodological terms, Castro harnessed the mobilization tactics of workers, students, businesspeople, and professionals, including strikes and demonstrations, culminating in the political general strike. He did not allow complete spontaneity, however; the MR 26-7 for the most part controlled all events.

The program outlined in Castro's "History Will Absolve Me" speech and other MR 26-7 documents described the long-standing agenda of reform demanded by Cuban society and served to mobilize all social sectors. Castro acted as the main propaganda agent, writing most of the official documents of the movement. He denounced the state, corruption, and the system as a whole to heighten the people's awareness, inspire faith in the emerging revolutionary movement, and gradually incorporate all patriots into the ranks of the MR 26-7.

Though the population as a whole lacked class consciousness, there was a certain solidarity among workers and peasants. A kind of popular opposition to all governments existed, due principally to the unemployment, illiteracy, lack of medical care, and poverty suffered by Cubans across the island. To a large extent, the population did not fully understand the social, historical, and scientific sources of their plight, attributing their condition to Batista or Grau San Martín or Prio's corrupt governments, which were stealing from the nation. Castro channelled this public discontent into his movement.[12]

* * *

In April 1955 the Cuban house of representatives passed an amnesty law covering all crimes against state powers and public order, without specific reference to the Moncada assailants. The FEU led the popular outcry demanding amnesty for the Moncada assailants. They were released in May.

A radio talk show in Matanzas played an important role in the pro-amnesty campaign. The organizers of the program invited several guests who were considered standard bearers of the constitution and the law. The military gave orders to cancel the meeting without considering the authorization given by the radio station's official ownership. In spite of these orders, a large group gathered at the station, and while the commentator was explaining why the show had been cancelled, an officer and several policemen arrived and arrested those present. Clashes such as these increasingly differentiated the military from the popular sectors.

Pro-amnesty street actions and demonstrations took place within the framework of acts of sabotage, sugarcane burnings, and labor strikes. Among the sugarcane fields burned were the Alava sugar mill of Gulf Atlantic in Colón, the San Julián and Las Mercedes farms, and the Tinguaro sugar mill. Two hundred *caballerías* were destroyed in the Zorrilla sugar mill of the Agrícola Retiro, a loss of some $16,000. And at Martín Rubio's Santa Lucía farm, rebels burned 40 *caballerías* of grazing lands. There were also strikes in the Araujo sugar mill of Manguito and in Coliseo's Carolina sugar mill.[13]

In the western part of the island, the MR 26-7 was reorganized throughout the provinces, municipalities, factories, and school centers. Its main task was to prepare for a popular uprising and war. In the first meeting of the Moncada assailants held in Havana, Israel Tápanes of Matanzas was instructed to start preparing for rebellion in his city.[14]

In June Castro began a political-economic and ideological campaign in the pages of the *Bohemia* magazine. The ostensible purpose of his diatribes was to collect funds to reopen *La Calle* newspaper, previously seized by the government. But his real purpose was to show that it was not possible to solve the country's crisis through the electoral option promoted by the opposition, since the regime would not give them sufficient space. The official organization of the MR 26-7 in Matanzas occurred later that summer. Ortodoxo sugar workers' leader Jaime López, Juan Manuel Torres, Ismael Pérez Falcón, Ricardo González Trejo, Pedro Miret, Ñico López, and Armando Hart met with Castro, who told them about how the 1895–1898 revolution had been thwarted by U.S. military intervention and how this was repeated in 1933; the true Cuban revolution, Castro said, still had to be won. When they arrived in Matanzas, López met with the Ortodoxo youth while González Trejo, Cuchi Torres, and Falcón began to organize in Jovellanos. The network of cells Muñoz had created in the territory of Colón in 1952 continued under Universo Sánchez.[15]

The group of future *Granma* expeditionaries went into exile, setting up revolutionary clubs in the United States. The main activities of the exiles were to organize, proselytize, collect funds, secure supplies, and train in the hope of "being free or martyrs in 1956."

As an offshoot of the Ortodoxos, the MR 26-7 prepared in Mexico for the expedition, taking up the doctrine of Chibás and the argument that it was not a political but a revolutionary moment. At the same time, in August 1955, the Ortodoxo Party sponsored rallies to commemorate the anniversary of the death of Chibás in Havana and held a national assembly that met in the Martí Theater. MR 26-7 delegates also attended. Their objective was to define the party line in favor of insurrectional struggle and the revolution. The Matanzas delegation included Ortodoxo Aldo Santamaría of La Rayonera, who had replaced Jaime López as chief of the MR 26-7 in the province, and the former member of the Auténticos, González Trejo. Eduardo Corona presided over the assembly.

The Martí Theater filled with people debating how best to remove Batista: through elections or armed struggle. MR 26-7 agitation groups were active inside. In the end, the majority favored the July 26 Movement's insurrectional program, the assembly crying out in chorus: "Revolution! Revolution!"[16] Armando Hart, a national MR 26-7 leader, read the assembly's agreements before the group marched to the cemetery to commemorate the fourth anniversary of the death of Chibás. The demonstration was disbanded by police forces with rifle and machine gun fire. The protesters burned and overturned police cars. Events like these in other places were similarly repressed.[17]

The MR 26-7 was strengthened in the Ortodoxo assembly in Havana and municipalities of Matanzas. Santamaría was already the provincial leader and operated from La Rayonera's industry areas and the workers' trade union, a stronghold of the MR 26-7. Its political composition was mostly leaders and members of the Ortodoxo Party and the Ortodoxo Youth.

The organization grew in size and strength after August 1955, aided by visits of national leaders to the provinces and the creation of action and sabotage worker and student Youth Brigades in workplaces and education centers.[18] All preparations focused on structuring the insurrection and the general political strike that was to take place once the *Granma* landing occurred. The MR 26-7 expanded its conspirational network and provided guidelines and instructions. Initially, the members of the national leadership also did conspiracy work together with the provincial chiefs, including Manuel Piñeiro; the Moncada assailant Israel Tápanes; Universo Sánchez, chief of the region of Colón; Ricardo González Trejo, chief of the Jovellanos region; Manuel del Cueto, chief of the Cárdenas region; and Puchín Montejo and Luis Avila of the Unión de Reyes region. The local offices of the FPTT and the provincial CTC served as meeting places. That the province was preparing for an uprising in support of the *Granma* landing was reflected in propaganda seized by the government. The slogan "Only Solution: General Strike and Insurrection" appeared repeatedly.[19]

The province of Matanzas joined the national telegraph workers' strike August 18–19, 1955, closing down mail and telegraph offices in the cities of Matanzas, Cárdenas, and Colón. Héctor Ponte, member of the MR 26-7 in Matanzas, was able to paralyze the telegraph department.[20]

While this was taking place during the summer of 1955, sisal workers, led by the telegraph workers' trade union, resumed their strike, which also included sabotage against the regime at the Jovellanos cordage company, La Cordelera Nacional, La Rayonera industry in Matanzas, Entidad Agapito Laurrari in Cárdenas, Las Carboneras farm, and the Henequenera Laurrari of Limonar. Strikes and acts of sabotage also hit Cubana de Gomas in Matanzas and the Fábrica de Hilazas Sintéticas of San José farm, Corral Nuevo. Sugar workers as well intensified their strikes in several sugar mills, including the Araujo in Manguito, the Carolina in Coliseo, the Arrechabala industry, La Vizcaya distillery, the San Nicolás distillery, the Licorera de Cárdenas, and the Aurora Distillery of Benito Pérez Hernández.[21]

From exile, Castro followed the increase in strikes throughout the country and wrote to Germán Castro Porta about the importance of these strikes in the MR 26-7 revolutionary strategy. He mentioned that the success of "any revolution or war" depended mainly on the strategy adopted and that "in the same revolutionary process, not all political groups may apply the best strategy," since this depended essentially on the role they had "played in public life and the social interest they represented." He specifically outlined the MR 26-7 view that the only possible way to overthrow Batista's dictatorship was through "an armed insurrection, backed by a revolutionary general strike and full sabotage" of all systems of communication throughout the island during the armed struggle. He believed that the success of the revolutionary strategy was to be found in exposing the conditions of the telegraph workers and bank workers on strike and the killing of the workers at the Washington sugar mill."[22]

Meanwhile, the provincial MR 26-7 leadership in Matanzas selected individuals to be trained in Mexico. José Smith Comas was among them. He immediately stood out in practices and was chosen chief of one group. The Matanzas contingent also included Horacio Rodríguez, Armando Huao, and "El Guajiro" Crespo.

During that period, the rural guard and state authorities were constantly reporting sugarcane field burnings, sabotage against railroads, and bombings. In Pedro Betancourt burnings occurred in the *colonias* of Amparo, Naranjo, and El Tejar.[23] Several acts of sabotage took place in June, on the occasion of a visit by Batista to Colón and Manguito to attend meetings. Forces of the SIR's Plácido Regiment and of Matanzas garrison discovered a bomb with several pounds of hooked nails on the Jagüey farm of the type that had been used against the president's motorcade. Matanzas telephone lines were also cut several times during this period.

Scores of workers were arrested between May and December 1955 for stealing the gear levers from urban buses of Matanzas. Port workers failed to report to their jobs. Workers paralyzed the yarn factory production. Parallel though not related to the activities of the MR 26-7's action and sabotage brigades, strikes began intensifying in December 1955, as workers demanded payment of the sugar price difference. Several workers' leaders were tried and imprisoned. Forty-three workers at the Arcos de Canasí sugar mill did not go to work and were arrested. In the Conchita mill of Alacranes, 110 workers were arrested. In the Santo Domingo mill in Unión de Reyes and the Progreso and Carolina sugar mills and sugarcane plantations in Cárdenas, repair works stopped as a result of union actions. There were also strikes supporting sugarcane workers, and shops closed down in many of these locations. The working class had become more aware of the need to resist the regime through armed struggle and the general strike.

After 1955 the MR 26-7's workers' leaders began playing an important role in several sectors. In highway cargo transportation, the Batista coup strengthened the owners' position against the workers, which provoked an internal struggle within the trade union movement. The trade unions that were able to keep their revolutionary leadership or because of member pressure could not remain aligned with Mujal's federation started moving toward an insurrectionist position. A group of Ortodoxo trade union leaders of the transportation sector, supporters of rebellion, started earning the trust of the rank and file. Traffic and transportation drivers decided to strike against the abuses committed against them. Many were arrested, and several groups were taken to Havana's Castillo del Príncipe prison; replacement workers were brought in to keep the trucks moving.

The Ortodoxo group in this trade union movement stood out, and many became MR 26-7 leaders. The MR 26-7's workers' section of the national highway and cargo transport trade union organized a large network of cells made up of men and women working in dispatch centers, cargo trucks, and mechanic shops that covered seventy-two enterprises, including Express Services Amaro, La República, La Cubana, and Tráfico y Transporte.

The underground network and actions developed within those sectors in which workers had lost all confidence in trade union leaders who served management. Thus, the most important task of the MR 26-7's labor leaders was to agitate and guide them in setting up "revolutionary committees" at workplaces. They also prepared press releases denouncing the activities of the industry, for a group of transportation company owners had begun to work with members of the regime to create a monopoly. The Interamerican Company that was established bought more than thirty enterprises through state money lent to private individuals. Although the movement could not stop the creation of the highway transport monopoly, worker pressure did prevent layoffs. The monopoly was

consolidated in 1956, and management appointed as director Sergio
Ferrer, a pro-government man well known to the workers of Autobuses
Modernos for having promoted massive layoffs in that enterprise.[24]

* * *

The MR 26-7 started to make important structural readjust-
ments during 1957. Besides cells at the provincial level, regional
cells were created in five territories: Matanzas, Jovellanos, Cárdenas, Colón, and Unión de Reyes. The national leadership for-
warded all work plans to the provincial coordinator and head of action, who then passed them along to regional heads.

As provincial chief, Aldo Santamaría, a member of the national
leadership, in practice operated as the head of the Matanzas region.
During the preparations for the *Granma* landing, Santamaría and
other regional leaders and combatants sought weapons, dynamite,
and anything available to add to their war materiel.

Agitation and propaganda work intensified. Press censorship
and suspension of constitutional guarantees, in force most of the time,
led to increased underground propaganda work. More articles appeared in foreign papers, mainly in the United States and Mexico,
where most of the earliest information on the anti-Batista struggle had
been published. In addition to confiscating leaflets and other propaganda, in August 1956 the police and the SIM seized a crucial document regarding the MR 26-7's strategy, tactics, and program in different municipalities and regions of the province. Part of the movement's
recruitment campaign, the manifesto was addressed "To Workers," its
title page reading, "The Workers Have Lost 500 Million Pesos. People:
Fight for Your Revolution! General Strike–Armed Insurrection." The
manifesto declared that once the movement earned national prestige
and put forth its message of struggle, "the great revolutionary mission
of the Cuban proletariat" would be to solve the people's social and
economic problems. The workers' presence in the general strike and
agitation was indispensable to guarantee the revolution, the manifesto
said, and the MR 26-7 would coordinate all preparations for both insurrection and the strike, since the March 1935 strike had failed because it had not combined the two methods.[25]

Acts of sabotage and other insurrectionary activities led by national chief Frank País became systematic and widespread in
Matanzas in late 1956. The head of the Western Railways station
denounced sabotage in the yards of the station of the Conchita
sugar mill in Unión de Reyes that derailed a locomotive. The same
happened to locomotives of the Progreso sugar mill. Meanwhile,

the action brigades of Matanzas sabotaged the railway branches of Jovellanos in the railroad's main yard. Incendiary materials were placed in public areas like the theaters of Calimete, Perico, Cárdenas, and Matanzas. A shed of the construction company employed by the government was burned in Unión de Reyes. Two young *fidelistas* were charged with burning sugarcane fields, distributing July 26 manifestos, and entering a house where a family was having a party, crying out "Long live Fidel Castro!"[26]

A group of Matanzas insurrectionists were accused in court of "having agreed with elements led by Dr. Fidel Castro from Mexico" to disturb public order and place bombs in the city. The Ortodoxo youth leader Leonel Güedes and Justino Baró, a member of the MR 26-7 student action brigade, were accused by the police of placing MR 26-7 stickers in the park of the Pueblo Nuevo church. Antonio Rodríguez of Versalles was arrested for distributing July 26 manifestos in the Libertad park in the center of the city reminding the people that "on August 12, 1933, the tyrant Machado had been overthrown," for which the July 26 youth brigades vowed that "the dictator Batista" would fall in 1956.[27]

The police pursued groups who put up stickers and painted walls with antigovernment slogans. Throughout the city of Matanzas, they seized pledges of insurrection in behalf of MR 26-7, recruitment forms, and forms to collect money. Police detective Ciro Hernández in August 1956 summarized the intensive propaganda activity of the insurgent organization during 1955–1956, which aimed at "using violence against state powers," as shown in the large number of cases "against several individuals known as activists and members of the constantly mentioned insurrectional group called the July 26."[28] In the Soledad sugar mill of Jovellanos, the leaflets signed by the MR 26-7 declared that after "four years of tyranny" during which hundreds of political crimes had been committed and workers' rights and salaries violated, the situation demanded and justified revolution.[29]

With the growing distribution of subversive leaflets in October and November 1956, sabotage at railway yards and in sugarcane fields increased. In the town of Banaguises, a boxcar owned by Ferrocarriles Occidentales de Cuba was burned.[30] In mid-November a bomb was placed at the residence of Perico's mayor.

* * *

The movement's provincial leadership in Matanzas, together with the regional leadership in Jovellanos, planned an attack on the

rural guard's garrison of that municipality to coincide with the expeditionary landing. It was to be carried out by 120 members of
Jovellanos action and sabotage groups and receive the support of
the action brigades of Matanzas, to be deployed near the military
squadron to keep the Plácido regiment from aiding in the defense
of the Jovellanos garrison. The MR 26-7 planned to send a truck
full of dynamite to blow up an outpost of the Matanzas garrison,
thus stopping troop movement to Jovellanos. A few months before
November 30, 1956, the provincial leader provided the rebel
brigades with weapons with which to practice. For its part, the region gathered together the first group of fighters and sent them
grenade shells, but they had to wait for the explosives that the
provincial leadership expected to obtain through Frank País, the
national action chief in Oriente, and detonators from the Pinar del
Río mines.

País planned to get firearms in Oriente through the movement's worker section at the Guantánamo Naval Base, for which a
few thousand dollars had to be collected as soon as possible. Initially, they thought of obtaining the money by requesting $500
from *colonos* and industrialists. They visited Mario Cuba, co-owner
of the Gravi sisal industry, which had already spent millions in propaganda because "Batista had to be eliminated, since the economy
was failing and that affected them." But once the regional leadership met with him, he said that he was not sure about the possibility of overthrowing the regime. The money was collected among
workers, the middle classes, and opposition doctors.[31]

But the weapons were never bought. When Aldo Santamaría
arrived in Oriente, País told him that there were still too many un-
armed men in the eastern province, where the landing was to take
place. Although the leadership of Jovellanos began procuring
weapons on its own, it was practically impossible to obtain all they
needed to implement their projects.

In late November 1956, Santamaría traveled to Havana to request instructions and obtain ammunition, firearms, and dynamite.
Regional chiefs had already been informed that the *Granma* landing
was to take place within seventy-two hours and that they should establish daily contact with the municipalities through the local FPTT-
CTC offices to implement the plans the province was responsible
for at zero hour, including derailing trains, cutting telegraph and
telephone communication and energy lines, closing down shops,
sabotaging the main industries, and paralyzing the country's economic life.[32]

He was expected that night by the provincial leadership in Matanzas, but he did not return; he had been arrested in the early hours of November 30. The national leadership reacted rapidly. Enrique Hart Dávalos immediately replaced Santamaría with the chief of the Jovellanos region. Once he assumed the provincial leadership, González Trejo left with orders for Matanzas.

Once González Trejo arrived in Matanzas, he went to the offices of the telegraph workers' trade union, using it as a base for instructions to the regions. After some time and because of security risks—whenever there was any opposition movement, the regime rapidly attacked and took over trade unions—he transferred the center of operations to the home of Elio Díaz and then to the home of Laudelino González.[33]

The national campaign for weapons and supplies for the November 30 actions in the west was thwarted. Most of the money collected in the country had been sent to Mexico to guarantee Castro's success in preparing the expedition that had to return in 1957 as the movement had promised the people.

Despite the difficulties that emerged in the territory as a result of shortages of war supplies, several successful actions did take place. The burning of sugarcane fields remained the preferred form of sabotage in the region. In Colón alone, 5,000 *arrobas* of cane were burned during the days of the landing (see Table 4.1). In the Alava mill, Onelio Alvarez was charged with burning and destroying a crane, belonging to the "July 26 insurrectional movement," and committing the crime of "obeying direct orders from Fidel's followers."[34]

Rayon workers' action brigades sabotaged the main water supply of La Rayonera, affecting 50 percent of the plant's production; Hedges threatened the workers with a total shutdown if sabotage continued. In the sisal industry and plantations, important machine parts were destroyed at La Fé farm in Cárdenas.[35] In Jarcía railroad worker Franklin Gómez and Rolando Sandarán, members of the action and sabotage front, exploded bombs in the railway while different antigovernment activities were held by the sisal workers' sector in the region of Cárdenas and Coliseo. The action and sabotage brigades that had trained in shooting billeted in the regions and municipalities of Matanzas, Cárdenas, and Jovellanos.

Some sixty members of the Jovellanos action and sabotage groups were deployed in the woods of La Fermina farm, a few miles from the city, from where they prepared to interrupt travel on the central tracks of the east-west railroad. They blew up the

Table 4.1 Sugarcane Field Burnings, January 1956

Municipality	Owner	Caballerías	Value
Manguito	Caney 1 farm	700,000	$12,600
Manguito	Caney 2 farm	700,000	7,000
Manguito	Colonia El Rocio	400,000	25,000
Colón	San Martín farm	15,000	600
Máximo Gómez	El Delilio farm	25,000	—
Máximo Gómez	San Antonio farm	300,000	16,000
Palmillas	Jicotea 2 farm	—	300
Palmillas	Jicotea 2 farm	20,000	2,000
Amarillas	La Juanita farm	40 000	2,800
Jovellanos	El Coronel farm, Cañera Matanzas Company	70,000	—
Jovellanos	Colonia Mulata	15,000	500
Jovellanos	Cañera Matanzas Company	1 cab.	1,000
Jovellanos	Colonia Criollera	10,000	—
Carlos Rojas	Colonia San Caudio	12,000	700
Total		2,307,000	68,780

Source: Provincial ACC Files, Matanzas, Fondo Tribunal de Urgencia, File 157, Nos. 10, 12, 14, 16, 18, 21, and File 158, Nos. 5, 7, and 8.

post that resulted in the collapse of telegraph communications with the entire island. Incendiary devices using chlorate and other materials were also placed in public places by action and sabotage brigades in locations like the theaters of Calimete, Perico, Cárdenas, and Matanzas.

During November–December 1956, Antonio Verdayes, an outstanding Ortodoxo sisal workers' leader in Coliseo and Cárdenas who had joined the MR 26-7 workers' section, was killed by the regime: Police forces bombed his residence at Limonar, intending to create confusion among the insurgents.

One of the most effective and systematic workers' insurgency groups was the action and sabotage group of El Cocal and El Bolo neighborhoods in Matanzas. It was made up mainly of the Gil Perdomo brothers and workers from the Cuban Electric Company—specialists in national communication lines in Matanzas Province. Better known as the *pica-postas* (pole cutters), they carried out numerous successful sabotage actions against power lines and telegraph and telephone communications, leaving the people of Matanzas and other regions of Las Villas Province cut off from the rest of Cuba.[36]

Although the regime sought to minimize the importance of the *Granma* landing and although the fighters of the Matanzas underground network lacked the weapons necessary to attack the regime's military positions, the network operated through sabotage actions on November 30 and continued operating all through December.

The MR 26-7's provincial coordinator believed that the movement's objective in Matanzas was to "do things that could intensify in a very short period," hold strikes, and force "the government to abandon power." There had been no underground in the province as such November 30. Underground life began on that day.[37]

* * *

Increased confrontations between the people's sectors and the government in 1955–1956 established the basis for civil war in Cuba. The cases filed against insurrectional elements from all social strata, workers, and students increased. The same happened in a number of municipalities, sugar mills, *colonias,* and farms, where elements or groups were accused of conspiring against the government or participating in sabotage actions, possessing weapons, and having other war materiel and propaganda.

In June 1956 workers of the Tinguaro mill, backed by the trade union, went on strike and refused to load sugar in the port of Cárdenas until overproduction was paid. Authorized by the trade union's secretary-general, the workers of the Tinguaro mill once again went on strike in September. The delegate of the sugar workers' federation participated; fifteen operators and switch tenders were arrested. Workers of the Betroma shoe distributing company also went on strike for economic reasons. That year the courts registered eighteen cases involving illegal possession of weapons.[38]

Action, sabotage, and propaganda activities became so serious that under the instructions of Colonel Pilar García the entire resources of the SIR were mobilized. The intelligence service arrested the members of the MR 26-7 brigade in El Cocal and El Bolo who had conducted several important actions. The government accused Castro of guiding these actions from abroad and of damaging the railway between Argüelles and Villamar. CMGW radio station was charged with insulting Batista in broadcasting a trade union recovery program against "the dictator, government collaborators, and CTC leaders" and making demands of the sugar industry workers' sector.[39]

Sabotage continued. On November 30, 1956, at the Jarcía Company of Matanzas on the San Rafael farm, workers rendered immobile the cordage factory's engines, thus impeding all plant activities. The cables of the Cuban Electric Company and army telephone lines were cut between Cárdenas and Cidra, around the Cinco Hermanos farm. Saboteurs sawed down power poles between Matanzas and Cárdenas in Arangueren and Carretera de Dubroy, Versalles. Losses amounted to $1,200. The insurrectional workers' cell of the Cubana Rayonera placed a bomb in industrial machinery. Eliseo Vera and Clemente Domínguez were arrested; the army seized explosives, a detonator, and a wick at Domínguez's home. According to the trial records, Rolando Muñiz, a member of the movement, ordered the action. Also implicated in these events as MR 26-7 leaders were Aldo Santamaría (already in prison in Havana), Angel Pérez Leyva, Gilberto Farías, Hugo García, Joaquín Torres, and Ricardo González Trejo.[40] The purpose of the action was to paralyze the workers' sector in the cordage industry and instigate a general strike. Hugo García Morales, an electrical appliances shopowner in Jovellanos, was charged as the MR 26-7 liaison with González Trejo, leading the July 26 Movement and being in charge of sabotage actions in that area. Four Mexican hand grenades were found in his car.[41]

Between December 1 and 11, the *pica-postas* toppled thirty-three of the Jovellanos–Colón utility poles and the Jovellanos–Carlos Rojas poles, interrupting power for several hours. Lines of the Juan Gualberto Gómez telegraph network were cut at Cidra; telephone and telegraph lines also cut at Manguito between Manguito and La Vega farm.

While *Granma* expeditionaries arrived at the Sierra Maestra on December 2, workers' action brigades in Matanzas were sabotaging the Jovellanos–Pedro Betancourt line in the Plantanal neighborhood. On December 3 they cut down two more poles of the Jovellanos–Jagüey Grande line at the María Luisa farm of the Isabel neighborhood. And on December 8 the local officer of the Cuban Electric Company reported that the poles of the Jovellanos–Jagüey Grande line, Cafetal farm, Isabel neighborhood, had been cut.

The movement's cell at the Becerra and Alvarez sisal plant performed acts of sabotage on December 3, forcing the plant to close down for repairs. Sabotage against a Matanzas–Unión de Reyes train occurred on December 11, together with actions against the Matanzas Arece Bank and others. In Cárdenas a group of students from the secondary education institute took to the streets and threw Molotov cocktails, burned a car tire, and stopped traffic by tossing glass and stones onto the pavement; Roberto Febles, a member of the MR 26-7 youth action brigades, was wounded and captured. In Matanzas the police arrested the Gil Perdomo brothers of the brigade of El Cocal and El Bolo. In searching their home, they found dynamite sticks, wicks and detonators, and subversive propaganda. The raid included the Vieja Bermeja neighborhood in San Antonio de Cabezas, Alcranes, where authorities arrested Rubén and Humberto Daría.[42] Aroldo Freire and Nicolás and Manuel Falcón Amaro of the Atrevido farm of Pedro Betancourt, all members of the neighborhood's action and sabotage group of the MR 26-7 region of Jovellanos, were charged with obeying orders of businessman Hugo García, from Carlos Rojas, who was also under arrest.

The report signed by the chief of investigation, Colonel Orlando Piedra Negueruela of the national police force, regarding the house search and arrest of the provincial MR 26-7 chief, González Trejo, highlights the coordinated efforts between the capital's repressive agencies and those of Matanzas Province. However, the police failed to arrest the movement's provincial coordinator.

In the police raids against inns and hotels, where they checked registration lists, they were unable to find the fugitives. In Ceiba Mocha the police searched the home of the movement's member Pablo García Lorenzo at the Camino Real of El Conde farm, a rural area under Arturo Lantigua, chief of the MR 26-7 action and sabotage in Ceiba Mocha; they discovered subversive leaflets supporting the July 26 Movement, calling for a general strike and armed insurrection.

Rural guard captain Cecilio Fernández arrested several MR 26-7 members in Matanzas for possession of firearms and other crimes, such as recruiting youth, distributing firearms supplied by Aldo Santamaría to be used against the armed forces, and "supporting the revolutionary movement that broke out in Santiago de Cuba, whose chief was Fidel Castro." Among other people involved in these actions were Luis Martínez, Rolando Hernández, and Wilfredo Mayor, from whom illegal firearms were confiscated. José Santiesteban, chief of the judiciary police, concluded that all were members of the "insurrectional organization called July 26" and that group chiefs in Matanzas Province were acting in cooperation with other elements conducting similar acts all over the nation, with the sole purpose of overthrowing the government.[43]

A significant arrest was that of Fidel Falla Bonet, a priest of the San Pedro Apóstol parish, for it revealed the degree to which the movement's network had penetrated the religious sector. Inside a hidden platform behind the main altar of the church, the police found several boxes containing war materials, including eighty-five hand grenade covers with detonators, 200 mercury detonators, and ten dynamite sticks. The police linked Rolando Muñiz with this action, charging him with being the MR 26-7 delegate in La Rayonera and collecting money from insurgent workers to promote a revolution and overthrow the government. At his trial prosecutors also said that by the time a hand-grenade plant had been discovered in Guanabacoa, 200 of the grenades had been given to Falla Bonet to be hidden in the parish.

Other MR 26-7 members were arrested in the December 1956 raids and charged with bombing several industries to paralyze them, attacking people, declaring a general strike, and taking up weapons against police forces, thus cooperating with the insurrectional movement that began in Oriente Province. The fighters were accused of "promoting a revolution to overthrow the established government." Authorities also charged that the money collected among workers "was being sent to Fidel Castro as head of the July 26 Movement."

Government agencies concluded that the action plan for November 30 in Matanzas involved placing "a tremendously powerful explosive device" in Matanzas city hall to force the police to leave the building, destroying the building as they had done in Santiago de Cuba, and promoting a revolutionary strike. On November 30, 1956, all military branches of the regime became aware of the extent of the July 26 network, its influence on the people, and the leadership of Fidel Castro in favor of insurrection and a revolutionary general strike to overthrow the Batista government.

5

Armed Struggle, Workers, and Guerrilla War

After the *Granma* landing, the MR 26-7 national leadership was assumed by Frank País. In 1956 País served as national delegate of action and sabotage, charged with preparations for armed struggle in all six provinces to support the expedition.

In December 1956 Fidel Castro directed País and Faustino Pérez to tour the island for the purpose of restructuring the movement by sectors on a national level. The role of the provincial coordinators was to organize, lead, and guide all other sectors, including action and sabotage, workers, finances, and propaganda. In 1957 País developed an independent movement, the Civic Resistance Movement (Movimiento Resistencia Cívica; MRC), to prepare and train workers, professionals, and businesspeople throughout the country in the use of the strike as a method of struggle. The workers' section, the MRC, and the National Students' Front (Frente Estudiantil Nacional; FEN)—also created in 1957—were to lead various social sectors in workplaces, student centers, municipalities, and provinces to a general strike across the island, backed by the military wing of MR 26-7.

Armando Huao, head of action and sabotage in Matanzas, and Joaquín Torres, coordinator of the workers' section, ordered the leadership of both sectors in regions and municipalities to coordinate all action plans. In Havana País and Pérez met with Ricardo González Trejo to instruct him on how the province should operate. After an exchange of views of the activities of the underground structure, González Trejo returned to Matanzas and organized the province's political-military division into five regions: Matanzas, Cárdenas, Colón, Jovellanos, and Unión de Reyes.

Prior to the *Granma* expedition, the Matanzas structure was directed by a provincial leader and a chief of action and sabotage, both linked to the municipal leadership. The provincial and regional leadership consisted of a general coordinator in charge of all projects, one workers' coordinator, one student coordinator, one in charge of finances, and one responsible for action and sabotage. Although a women's front did not exist as such, women played an important role. Despite the risk of being taken prisoner, tortured, or murdered, they assumed key responsibilities and served as regional and municipal coordinators and student activists and were prominent in propaganda and finance work.[1]

González Trejo was ratified as general coordinator after the reorganization of the MR 26-7 in January 1957. He was joined by Joaquín Torres of the Rayonera industry as workers' coordinator, and Armando Huao—one of the expeditionaries of the *Granma*—as head of action and sabotage. There was no student front at the outset. After its founding in May 1957, the FEN was led by Caridad Díaz Suárez. Reynaldo Avila was the head of propaganda, and the finance section was led variously by Raúl Cepeda, Israel Tápanes, and Veneranda Sánchez.[2]

The national leadership set the general guidelines, but these were subsequently adapted to the characteristics, conditions, and possibilities of the local regions and municipalities. Meetings were held regularly. Activities within the workers' sector were led by the provincial workers' front under the leadership of the national workers' coordinator.

The first memo País sent to all provincial leaders after his appointment in December 1956 analyzed the correlation of forces between the MR 26-7 and the Batista regime. In the document he outlined the general insurgent project to be implemented across the island. País examined the juncture of the organization and the independence struggle, which he described as "difficult" due to a lack of fighters. País believed that the situation in the aftermath of the landing of the *Granma*, however, had placed the government on the defensive, since "most of the people" in Santiago de Cuba were conspiring and relations between civilians and the military were tense. Conflicts seemed to have developed among Batista's followers. Internal command differences in the Maceo Regiment among Díaz Tamayo, Barreras, Labastida, Grao, and Casillas had reached into the ranks and local civilian politicians. The financial cost inflicted by acts of sabotage and war had reached $13 million, obliging the government to withdraw its troops from several localities in the eastern territory. At the same time, the extra hours of work the rebel attacks meant for government soliders were already creating unrest and discontent among the rank and file.

País reported that sabotage and other insurrectionary activities were occurring across the island, affecting the government far more than was being revealed. If the burning of sugarcane fields and the sabotage of sugar mills continued, the state's revenues would decline considerably. If sabotage extended into the beginning of the harvest, with the costs this implied, the situation of the government would become desperate. Besides sabotage against sugarcane fields, País recommended actions against telegraph, telephone, and electric power systems; water pipes; public offices; stores; government residences; bridges; and highways: He advised the use of "many nails and Molotov cocktails."

The plan was to reproduce MR 26-7 bulletins and distribute them "as much as possible in their respective urban or rural areas." The leadership set up a committee to disseminate information to reporters and radio stations on any combatant captured by the government, in the hope that publicity would discourage the government from beating and torturing prisoners. Another committee was formed to visit prisoners and provide them with food, clothes, money, and medicine. But the MR 26-7 also suggested punishment for those who hindered, obstructed, or otherwise opposed the revolution. Such punishment was severe, and even included execution.

In his December 1956 circular, País urged all action group chiefs to coordinate their plans for sabotage and ordered the reorganization of all action cells to select the most capable leaders and concentrate the leadership into fewer hands, with a provincial chief to whom the national action leadership would distribute plans. País further urged that actions be undertaken carefully and rapidly with respect to workers, mainly sugar workers, and involve a general strike during the harvest, thereby halting all sugar mills and permitting workers who belonged to the movement to implement agitation campaigns. He did not want this to be postponed, since it was "as important as sabotage."[3]

Although the workers' section was organized within the movement in 1955, it was not efficiently structured throughout the country until País readjusted it at all levels in December 1956. País believed it was important to develop worker activity across the island, initially as a political general strike in support of the landing of the *Granma* and the November 30, 1956, uprising, thus implementing Castro's strategy.

The national managing committee established by railroad trade union leaders Ñico Torres and Octavio Louit generalized strike methods among provincial sections, made up mostly of Ortodoxo labor leaders who had promoted antigovernment action among trade unions since the 1952 coup. Torres and Louit worked to train and organize workers' cadres from the movement into a dynamic group capable of reaching the level of the revolutionary general strike.

In Guantánamo the large workplaces such as railroads and sugar mills were organized into departments and sections. Smaller workplaces were organized by areas, such as in stores, and by products, such as butcher shops. Torres prepared a guide to partial work stoppages and their duration, the reasons for stoppages, the workers' level of organization and support, and how to organize them in large or small workplaces or in the street by product areas.

Through partial stoppages, the MR 26-7 began training workers' cadres in Guantánamo during the insurrection's preparatory stage in 1955 and 1956. A number of workplaces supported the November 30 actions and the *Granma* landing with a political strike that lasted several days, was backed by sabotage, and prevented army and police forces from leaving the region to participate in the repression in Santiago de Cuba.[4] The Guantánamo experience taught the MR 26-7 how to force the government to disperse its forces: an armed popular uprising in urban and rural areas split the operations of the armed forces, obliging them to confront the guerrilla forces in the mountains on one hand and deal with the civic urban actions in their respective territories on the other.

In its role as a revolutionary political party, the MR 26-7 maintained this same project during 1957 and 1958, gradually weakening the capacity of the government to deal with the rebel army under the direct leadership of Castro. The underground-civic structure helped to undergird the military vanguard, which was the only force perceived capable of defeating the Batista regime's main support: the regular army.

Only in Guantánamo was this project implemented successfully, making it an organizational model. The popular classes remained on strike for several days during late November and early December, simultaneously supporting the action and sabotage and the newly emerging MR 26-7 rebel army. Ñico Torres believed the objective of the political strike was achieved in Guantánamo both in theory and practice because it did not involve workers' economic demands but took place simultaneously with armed actions throughout the region. That is, the people's insurrection in 1956 was successful because the strike was planned in a manner consistent with established practices, and armed actions were undertaken in conjunction with the strike. In the management committee, Octavio Louit operated as workers' coordinator in the provinces. He began organizing in Oriente and subsequently traveled to Camagüey, Las Villas, and finally into the western provinces.

País translated this newly acquired experience into practice and assigned the workers' section its dual role: (1) establishing a cell network in different sectors with sufficient strength to guarantee the political general strike as soon as popular insurrection developed and (2) teaching sabotage techniques against industrial plants and other sectors of manufacturing and production. He informed Castro that already in July 1957 the workers' provincial leadership in Oriente had its "municipal directors operating at full capacity," prepared to take on economic and propaganda work. País had started creating the structure for executive leadership in Oriente, Camagüey, and Santa Clara; other delegates were at that moment developing similar plans in Pinar del Río, Havana, and Matanzas.

It is important to assess País's evaluation of conditions at that moment. With respect to the workers' program, he planned to consolidate the workers' section and the MRC leadership, whereupon a strike committee would be formed. The task of the delegates was to bring together important civic, political, religious, and commercial leaders with workers' organizations in a strike committee to act in conjunction with the MR 26-7 leaders.

This served as the civilian foundation upon which the emerging party depended. Its strength consisted of "its active belligerence" and "workers' and resistance cadre," already with "a powerful strength," and it could under any circumstances "pursue the revolutionary path already planned." País made it clear that in the military front the workers' leadership had sabotage sections to support all national actions that were planned. Because of their crucial importance, "these sections were made up by MR 26-7 members."[5]

The MRC was created to attract professionals, businesspeople, intellectuals, and industrialists—people who could not otherwise be recruited to the movement as activists in conspiracy. These members of the higher social strata became sources of valuable and responsible leadership, to be trained to assist with the middle class in the dissemination of propaganda and collection of funds. All MRC plans had as their final goal the preparation of the movement's

social and military base by initiating brief work stoppages combined with actions and sabotage. Implementation of this work program, together with increased actions by the rebel army in the
Sierra Maestra, would promote popular awareness of the MR 26-7
and awaken the faith of the people in the capacity of MR 26-7 to
wage a successful revolutionary struggle against Fulgencio Batista.

In May País intensified organizing activities. In several circular
letters of the national leadership, his skills as a revolutionary became obvious. In his May 15, 1957, letter "to the comrades of the
July 26 leadership in the nation," his analysis concluded with the
recommendation to centralize and streamline the movement's leadership. This was important, for he believed that one of the difficulties prior to the *Granma* landing was the unwieldy nature of the
leadership and its inability to make decisions efficiently. He called
for the separation and specialization of all sectors, granting full au-
thority and responsibility to all sector chiefs and distributing tasks
in as organized a manner as possible to develop propaganda and
sabotage work and coordinate all actions nationally. That was the
key to his success as an organizer: to decentralize all commands
and concede to them control over daily affairs. In regard to the
cadre policy, he ordered that the positions of organizer, treasurer,
and leaders of workers' groups, action and sabotage, and propaganda should have substitutes named and prepared to step in at a
moment's notice.

A vital element of the MR 26-7 was its flexibility: Although
plans were drawn up on a national level, in practice they were
adapted "according to each region's peculiarities" and open to the
initiatives of commanders at all levels.[6] Since the movement was
not rigid in its plans, the intermediate cadres were also able to
apply them according to their area's specific conditions. And because of this lack of total uniformity in the movement's *modus
operandi,* the regime found it much more difficult to combat the MR
26-7 than traditional opposition parties.

País called on all coordinators to move rapidly to organize "the
methods of the movement and begin to draw up plans for all sections." He asked them as revolutionaries and ordered them as
members of a disciplined organization to make great efforts in their
future plans because of the importance to the final victory.[7]

The insurrectional wave gained momentum during the early
months of 1957. But the failed attack against the presidential palace
in 1957 resulted in great confusion within the MR 26-7 between
May and June. And although the government made mistakes,

including intervening in the trade unions in the summer of 1957, opposition elements often weakened themselves in fighting. In order to deal with the fragmented opposition and the lack of revolutionary ideals, País urged the establishment of ties with the "honest, courageous and revolutionary generation," gathering together all those sectors who "felt the need of a true revolution." In contrast to those opposition sectors that sought to negotiate understandings with the government, the MR 26-7 intended to address historic Cuban frustrations with original, all-encompassing economic, political, and social programs.

País expressed his desire "to defeat a dictatorship that stains our history as a people that loves liberty; to put an end to economic bankruptcy; to administer and live honestly; to recover liberty for the Cuban people." It was clear that "all MR 26-7 members had to take into consideration the century's political, economic, and social trends." País expressed his conviction that the MR 26-7 had to "deeply shake up all sectors of the nation" and create revolutionary plans to make these sectors work "for the benefit of the new *patria,*" which included overthrowing and destroying the colonial system, doing away with the old bureaucracy, eliminating superfluous government mechanisms, establishing true values that matched Cuba's "idiosyncrasies," introducing the predominant modern philosophical trends, and building a new nation. He insisted on the need to achieve "true ideological unity and full identity of purpose and principle" to allow coordinated efforts and provide guidance for all members. With respect to finances, it would be necessary to work more in the provinces and with the July 26 clubs abroad to accumulate the necessary funds.[8]

*   *   *

País and his project of setting up rebel fronts inspired the MR 26-7 leaders and members in Matanzas. People in Matanzas were proud of their history and especially their past participation in patriotic struggles, including the battles waged by the liberation army between 1895 and 1898. During the 1950s, they sought to organize the MR 26-7 as a liberation army in the province. The project included forming action and sabotage sectors around the smallest possible number of well-trained partisans, elaborating plans and implementing them rapidly, developing varieties of sabotage techniques, and maintaining the strictest discipline and organization, punishing those who informed to the authorities or were indiscreet in their personal conduct. Other goals involved expanding propaganda to increase the number of participants operating in rearguard activities, developing a network of safehouses to hide activists, and acquiring equipment.

Active action and sabotage brigades in Matanzas increased their armed assaults against public services and telephone and telegraph communications all through the first half of 1957, most notably under the leadership of workers employed by the electric company as technicians who operated underground and the so-called *picapostas*. One action brigade operating in Las Villas and Matanzas was especially effective in placing explosives and time bombs and in destroying bridges. In May the leadership instructed the brigade to carry out several sabotage actions from Las Villas to Colón as part of the preparations for the Cienfuegos uprising and the establishment of rebel groups in the Escambray mountains. In late May the group led by Julio Pino Machado placed time bombs in Santa Clara and then moved on to other Las Villas municipalities.[9]

But these were costly operations. Accidental explosions took the lives of Pino Machado and Chiqui Gómez Lubián. In Matanzas the command of the rural guard squadron and the Colón police seized the bomb factory and arrested Armando Capote and Amador del Valle; Gladys García was also captured by the authorities. Caridad Díaz went underground, and Diosdado Sarmiento went into exile.

These events galvanized the movement in Las Villas. Friends and schoolmates of Pino Machado and Gómez Lubián in the medical school joined the movement, wanting to become part of the brigade. Groups from different social sectors organized a demonstration at the funeral. Margot Machado, a provincial leader and comrade in arms of País, urged well-wishers not to send flowers but to give money for the cause. During the trial against Gladys García, students blocked traffic on the main highway where the city hall was located.[10]

These events occurred within a general plan originally sent to País by the revolutionary movement within the government armed forces. Despite the early arrest of thirty combatants in Cienfuegos, the rebels persisted, and several months later on September 5, the Cienfuegos naval rebellion took place. Rodolfo de Las Casas, an outstanding action and sabotage leader in Villa Clara, the provincial action chief Osvaldo Rodríguez, Emilio Aragonés of the Cienfuegos leadership, and José Quiala of the capital's action groups were taken prisoner.

One of the most successful operations of the action and sabotage brigades in Matanzas during this time was the burning of the Tinguaro mill at Los Arabos, which produced such a large fire that the plotters left the scene convinced that they had totally destroyed the mill. In fact, plantation owners, prepared for these acts of arson, had several fire-fighting units at their disposal. Nevertheless, vast quantities of sugar were destroyed in the warehouses, the losses reported at over $5 million.[11]

The confidential reports issued by Colonel Pilar García, chief of the Plácido Regiment, identified a group of provincial and regional leaders of the MR 26-7 in Colón as "insurrectional elements involved in sabotage actions" in the burning of the Tinguaro mill. In another report by Captain Fernández Suero, the army claimed that the "chief of the so-called July 26 insurrectional movement in the province was Ricardo González Trejo," who together with others had planned the burning of the mill and other sabotage actions, "thus cooperating with the insurrectional movement led by Dr. Fidel Castro that seeks to overthrow the government." The army further noted that the movement was organized through cells in Perico and the Tinguaro sugar mill to carry out actions that would have an "international impact."[12]

The Matanzas workers' brigades' actions against La Rayonera's electric structures certainly had a great—if not international—impact. The superintendent reported that when the patrolman of the Havana-Matanzas line reached the structure behind La Rayonera, he discovered a time bomb, which he reported to the rural guard.[13]

Court records reveal the magnitude and success of the underground network, for police authorities admitted that they were unable to arrest the people responsible for these actions because of their clever and careful preparations. In the region of Colón alone, rebels set fire to mailboxes using liquid phosphorus, sabotaged the property of the Western Railways, bombed, burned the local stadium, and cut communication lines at Los Arabos.[14]

Between May and June 1957, the rural guard reported the cutting of telegraph and telephone lines and destruction of the local railway facilities. The regional office of the Ministry of Communications in Jovellanos reported the cutting of local telegraph lines, interrupting service with Carlos Rojas, Cárdenas, Varadero, Máximo Gómez, and Martí. The foreman of the Cuban Electric Company reported that unknown people sawed down a pole at Pueblo Nuevo, resulting in a blackout. A private guard of the Havana Western Railways in Cárdenas reported a sabotage of the Cárdenas-Jovellanos branch and the derailing of a locomotive, the crane, and its host cart with materials, causing extensive damage and interrupting train traffic for several hours between Cárdenas and the Progreso mill.[15]

The plans País had developed proved successful in the Matanzas network. During the first half of 1957, members of the MR 26-7 carried out a major act of sabotage at the Santa Catalina estate in Perico, causing losses of $11,500. The action brigade spilled 375 gallons of the transformer's oil and burned a building in Roque on the property of the Cuban Electric Company, destroying a tractor, fertilizing equipment, a trailer, and a grain collector of the Ministry of Agriculture.

Subsequently arrested were municipal and regional leaders of Jovellanos and regional coordinator of MR 26-7 in Cárdenas Manuel del Cueto, identified as "the first chief of the national July 26 terrorist movement in Cárdenas," who, following orders of Fidel Castro and "taking advantage of his work as physical education professor of La Progresiva school, mobilized a group of young people to create a situation of uncertainty among the people of that area." All were sent to the provincial jail.[16]

In the summer of 1957, País ordered an intensification of action plans and short work stoppages. In Matanzas the *pica-postas* resumed their sabotage against communication lines, interrupting service between Camagüey, Oriente, and Las Villas in the east and Matanzas, Havana, and Pinar del Río in the west. They also destroyed the Coliseo communication lines, disrupting service between Jovellanos and Colón and between Colón and Los Arabos. At the same time, the students' action brigades in Cárdenas destroyed the building of the institute. Classes had to be discontinued. On July 26, the police seized an MR 26-7 flag in Matanzas and one in Jagüey Grande, where the post office of the town was set on fire with liquid phosphorus.[17]

On July 30, 1957, at the height of his organizational successes, Frank País, leader of the political-civic-military underground vanguard of the MR 26-7, was killed in an armed skirmish in Santiago de Cuba. The effects of País's death reverberated throughout the provinces. In Matanzas stores closed, rebels committed acts of sabotage, and students went on strike; in Cárdenas workers paralyzed the sisal industry. People at large took to the streets in joint actions, burning tires, cars, and buses. Local women's groups organized a demonstration to coincide with a visit of the U.S. ambassador to Santiago de Cuba, and members were attacked by police forces in his presence. The U.S. government prepared naval units for possible evacuation of U.S. citizens residing in the industrial and mining communities in the east.

From the eve of País's death until August 5, a revolutionary strike swept Cuba, accompanied by armed actions, sabotage, and popular mobilizations. At the outset the strike movement operated without the command's order. Soon René Ramos Latour assumed control from Santiago de Cuba. As the August strike expanded throughout the island, it marked another step forward in the people's awareness that a general strike could topple the regime. Discontent rose among the population, and the army's rearguard began to weaken.

* * *

Although the death of País was an irreparable loss for the movement and a blow to Castro, the MR 26-7 continued to carry out País's plans. País had established contact with military conspirators planning to overthrow Batista in coordination with the MR 26-7. The Cienfuegos uprising demonstrated País's abilities in fusing together plans of the various parts of the underground opposition and the effectiveness of combining the tactics of insurrection and strike. Although the joint uprising of the navy and other elements of the armed forces and the MR 26-7's military structure did not produce a nationwide insurrection, it demonstrated that it was possible to mobilize an entire city and that people responded to the MR 26-7's political message.

Cienfuegos was the first action by the armed forces in collaboration with the MR 26-7. The naval plot was led by Manuel San Román, former navy lieutenant; Julio Camacho, action chief of the MR 26-7 in Las Villas; and officers of the navy working at the naval base. MR 26-7 reinforcements wore olive green uniforms and MR 26-7 armbands and were armed by the main garrison of the base. The combined forces seized the maritime police post and the national police station. At the same time, the streets of Cienfuegos filled with demonstrators in support of MR 26-7 and the rebellious naval post.

The government responded immediately. Some 400 troops of the provincial regiment reinforced the soldiers defending the Cienfuegos military command and engaged the 200 MR 26-7 men. Together with 100 marines of the Cayo Loco Naval Base, the MR 26-7 combatants confronted the Villa Clara Regiment in a heavy gun battle. The troops of Matanzas military district led by Colonel del Valle attempted to assist the besieged forces in Cienfuegos but were repelled by the naval rebels and MR 26-7 combatants. Four tanks were ordered in to support the government forces. Colonel Fernando Rey did not "take one single civilian or naval wounded—only dead." The result was a massacre: more than 300 dead.[18]

In late 1957 Comandante Raúl Castro ordered the provincial leadership to step up sabotage against the 1958 harvest as a way to undermine the regime's economic base. In Matanzas MR 26-7 had large quantities of explosive materials obtained by an action group led by Armando Huao during the attack against the Corral Nuevo supplies warehouse. The stores were so extensive that Matanzas was able to supply other provinces.[19]

Sabotage at La Rosa farm in Jovellanos caused losses of $10,000; $1,000 of damage was done to the Dámaso López estate and $4,000 in León. In the San Claudio de Coliseo farm in Carlos Rojas, 100 *caballerías* were burned. Losses at the Triunfo sugar mill were estimated at $2,000; in the Colón region, 40 *caballerías* of the Columbia *colonia* valued at $5,000 were destroyed; 30 *caballerías* of La Vega farm worth $2,625 were burned in Alacranes; and 500 *caballerías* worth $40,000 were destroyed in the Atrevido farm in Bolondrón. Many other small fires were set in sugarcane fields near the highway connecting Unión de Reyes, Guines, Matanzas, and Bolondrón, carried out by flinging Ping-Pong balls loaded with chlorate and sulphuric acid from moving cars. Sabotage actions were taken against *colonias* in Cárdenas supplying the Dos Rosas mill, the Hires Sugar Company, the Progreso Sugar Company, and Guipúzcoa Company. More than fifty fires were reported in Jovellanos, where there was a strong action and sabotage organization among agricultural workers. Between November and December 1957, more than 3 million *arrobas* of cane were destroyed in the region of Unión de Reyes.[20]

The MR 26-7's campaign against the sugar industry in December 1957 created new tension between the Batista government and the large sugar interests. Under these circumstances, the alternative plan of a military junta to oust Batista, like that of 1933–1934, gained some adherents as a way to leave power in the hands of the military. In the face of this possibility, MR 26-7 accelerated preparations for a general strike to move against a military junta.

Government repression increased in severity and expanded in scope. In late 1957 the underground apparatus in Matanzas was destroyed with the repression of the armed forces under Pilar García's command. Government agents captured and murdered the provincial chief of action and *Granma* expeditionary Armando Huao and his replacement, Gilberto Espiñeira.

In November 1957 the national leadership ordered resumption of preparations for a general political strike that would eventually become known as the April 1958 strike. Because of the magnitude of the plan, the underground network was again reorganized in all regions. The forces favoring the insurgency of the people's sector gained strength in January and February 1958. Terror and repression increased, but so, too, did the opposition, and the belief in the eventual triumph of the revolution slowly took hold.

Enrique Hart Dávalos was appointed provincial chief of Matanzas in February 1958 upon leaving the Castillo del Príncipe prison in Havana. In Matanzas the plan for a revolutionary general strike and the orders of the national leadership originated from Commander Daniel, the national action chief, who conveyed them to Ricardo González Trejo and Enrique Hart. The orders were transmitted to the civilian sector and organized with regional action coordinators and chiefs. Guerrilla operations intensified from February to April as a way to support the militia units and armed patrols. Meanwhile, Joaquín Torres and Eliseo Camaño were sent by the national leadership to buttress the workers' structure in Matanzas and prepare for the general strike to be led by the workers' section. Strike committees, as originally conceived by Frank País, were created for the April 9 strike. The organization and development plan sent to all provinces indicated that the strike would be led by a national strike committee with headquarters in Havana. The committee, appointed by the national leadership, was made up of five people in charge of action, propaganda, labor, resistance, and organization. The leadership of the strike would be shared by the commander in chief of the MR 26-7 militia, headquartered in Santiago de Cuba, and the commander in chief of the rebel army, Fidel Castro. Provincial committees with a similar composition were established in all provinces and in many municipalities.[21]

* * *

The April general strike was the product of rebel groups (*focos*) that evolved fully into guerrilla detachments during the second half of 1958. In natural and logical fashion, they developed into a guerrilla force that by the end of 1958 extended across the entire island. Rebel groups were organized and expanded in Matanzas, Alturas de Madruga, Havana Province, around Corralillo, and along the Matanzas–Las Villas northern boundary. They were formed by members of action and sabotage groups drawn from urban and rural areas who had been "burned" (*quemados*), that is, identified by security forces, and therefore required to withdraw and organize into armed bodies in open rebellion.

Enrique Hart, provincial action chief, in collaboration with regional coordinators and action chiefs, implemented the plans of the MR 26-7 national leadership. These plans called for the combination of militia units with guerrilla detachments under an autonomous command unit. One of the principal objectives of the combined militia-guerrilla unit as outlined in the national strike plan was to cut communications lines and interrupt highway and railroad traffic.

Units organized for the April strike continued to operate in the regions of the provinces of Havana and Matanzas and along the Matanzas–Las Villas border. Two groups in Matanzas, the Ceiba Mocha–Madruga group, operating around Alturas de Matanzas and Madruga, and La Paciencia group, known as the *pica-postas* since the creation of the MR 26-7 in Matanzas, took up arms near the San Juan River. Since its inception in 1955, this group operated as an urban action and sabotage group in the area of El Cocal and El Bolo. During the entire period, their mission was to interrupt electrical service and telephone and telegraph communications.

Two groups operated in the region of Cárdenas: one at Loma Phinney between Cárdenas and Coliseo and the other in the Sierra de Bibanasí in the municipality of Martí. Las Piedras group operated in Colón and consisted of combatants from Bolondrón and Pedro Betancourt. A number of small groups were established around Corralillo groups on the border of the region of Colón and Las Villas Province and operated in Los Arabos, San José de los Ramos, and Colón. The groups Chiva Muerta and La Fermina in Jovellanos were made up of the urban and rural militia of the municipalities of Jovellanos, Agramonte, and Jagüey. Enrique Hart also incorporated to his provincial command Ignacio Fernández, previously a leader of the MR 26-7 in Jovellanos; Alejandro Sánchez Cervantes, militia chief from Havana; and Oscar Gutiérrez and Dagoberto Díaz, both from the regional action group of Cárdenas. This commando unit began operations during the first week of April, in line with the national plan of attacking transportation and halting highway traffic. Hart also traveled to Jovellanos to establish contact with Erelio Peña, regional action chief and leader of the local rebel group, to coordinate plans for the rebel uprising.[22]

One of the first significant actions involved an assault on the town of Miguel de los Baños on April 5. Wearing MR 26-7 armbands, the rebels occupied several buildings and subsequently departed. The Ceiba Mocha group led by Alicia Pérez Bello and action chief Arturo Lantigua prepared the uprising in the area south of Mocha and Cabezas, bordering Havana and San Fabián and Loma de Camarones in the heights of Madruga-Matanzas.[23] They played an important role in the operational unit at the Havana-Matanzas border. In early April the Madruga and Aguacate militia, upon learning of the strike, seized a portion of the main highway at the entrance of Matanzas coming from Madruga, interrupted traffic, and destroyed several motor vehicles. The *pica-postas'* action and sabotage activities led by Israel Gil Perdomo contributed to the creation of a revolutionary climate several days before the strike. The most important mission of the group was to signal the beginning of the April strike by cutting electricity and telephone and telegraph communications and halting traffic in the Cidra-Matanzas stretch of the main highway. Their only weapons were Remington rifles and pistols. At midnight on April 8, they cut all lines crossing La Paz, Las Cuevas, and San Juan, and those of the Rayonera Cubana, thus producing blackouts in Matanzas, Jovellanos, Coliseo, Colón, and Cárdenas.[24]

The main purpose of the Cárdenas action group was seizure of the dockyards and the airport. At the same time sisal workers' units were to interrupt highway traffic in Camarioca. All stores and hotels were to be closed at the moment of the strike. In Cárdenas and surrounding towns and sugar mills, the FON and labor sections would issue the call for the strike the day before. El Phinney rebel group was to sabotage the Cárdenas aqueduct, leaving the city without water, whereupon they were to raid the police station in support of the militia and distribute weapons to the people. In a joint operation, both MR 26-7 military forces would attack the army garrison.[25] Meanwhile, the MRC would take over city hall.

The strike order was not received in Cárdenas on April 8, but the day after. The coordinator heard the MR 26-7's radio announcement, saying: "Attention all Cubans! Attention all Cubans! This is July 26 calling for a revolutionary general strike! Today is the day of liberty! The day of the revolutionary general strike! All Cubans forward!"[26] The action chief of Cárdenas had organized two units of rebels, one in Loma Phinney and the other in Martí, which consolidated to operate around the Sierra de Bibanasí. The groups operated with the militia organized into action groups from the city of Cárdenas and nearby towns. Action groups from several neighborhoods burned tires on the streets to halt traffic while throwing leaflets, nails, and liquid phosphorus. One group made up of militiamen and rebels was given the mission of stopping traffic by pouring oil and petroleum on the Cárdenas-Coliseo highway near El Phinney hill.

The uprising of Las Piedras south of Bolondrón near the area of the Zapata swamps was under the command of Raúl Trujillo, the coordinator of the region of Colón. The regional leaders in Cárdenas and Güira de Macurijes were the contact elements of this group.

The day before the strike action, units were ordered to attack government positions. But plans went awry. In Jovellanos the plan to take over the local garrison was abandoned because of the shortage of arms. The unit decided to divide into small groups and function as mobile commandos, undertaking hit-and-run operations. The group from Agramonte joined the militia led by coordinator Emérito García and operated both in the town as well as the surrounding countryside, attacking local sugar mills and disrupting mill operations. One brigade paralyzed the San Ignacio mill for three days by damaging the rail spur. The rebel group from Los Freyre loosened rails of the line from Havana to Coliseo and Jovellanos and cut telephone lines with machetes.[27]

In Corralillo the strike plans of the MR 26-7 national leadership were successfully implemented. The local militia received timely information that enabled the combatants to put into practice the combined military action, guerrilla action, and the strike. Militia units and rebels together seized the Corralillo garrison, forcing the soldiers to withdraw. MR 26-7 leaders organized the popular defense units by establishing sentries and patrols, thereby preventing surprise attacks by army troops from Sagua la Grande and the Matanzas regiment. The defense was organized along access roads and highways and an observation post established on a church spire, the highest point in town. The uprising generalized throughout the Corralillo municipality and its surroundings. The MR 26-7 maintained control over the government forces from April 9 to 11, when the government counteroffensive began.[28]

The MR 26-7 municipal leadership had been convinced they controlled the town and were certain that the final offensive had been launched and the end of Batista was at hand. It was only when they heard programs from Havana on battery-powered radios that they realized the situation in the island was normal and that the strike had failed.[29]

By early May the government had restored order in Cárdenas. Many of the principal urban leaders had been killed and arrested. Systematic repression followed.[30]

In the aftermath of the abortive strike, almost all provincial units were reorganized and redeployed. The only group that subsequently remained as an organized force was that of Agramonte. It continued to evolve and develop all through 1958, and was structured as the Luis Avila Detachment. Members of other rebel groups from Jovellanos joined the Mario Muñoz Detachment in Colón. Others left the region to join the Escambray Front in Las Villas or a new center of armed operations in Pinar del Río.

The underground structure, however, continued to maintain harassment operations. After the appointment of a new action chief, militia units reorganized. The MR 26-7 united the provincial leadership with the armed groups in the cities of Cárdenas, Máximo Gómez, Martí, Itabo, Varadero, Camarioca, Guásimas, and Cantel and local mills. Under the slogan "Unity at the base," they established contact through the local chief of the civic resistance, Enrique Sáez, with the AAA and the March 13 DR representative. Labor leader Raúl Lago had attempted to do the same with the Popular Socialist Party (Partido Socialista Popular) but did not succeed.[31]

Once the MR 26-7 decided that it was impossible for the national leadership to supply the rebel groups with weapons and ammunition, they informed combatants that they should obtain weapons on their own, by taking weapons from anyone who owned arms. They also planned an attack against La Cordelera industry in Cárdenas to disarm the guards.

Repression increased from April to May. Auténtico elements that rebelled with the MR 26-7 at El Phinney hill abandoned the area for Havana. During the summer the less "burned" combatants went into the cities; those most "burned" remained in the field, conducting rural operations in and around the same territory where they operated during preparations for the April strike. The group of El Phinney carried out their operations in the region of Cárdenas, operating as the Enrique Hart guerrilla detachment, and subsequently joined the column with the same name formed under the leadership of Captain Juan R. López Fleites. During the last month of the insurrection, it operated in the area of the Guamacaro Valley, Coliseo, and San Miguel, where the column had its headquarters.

Part of the Corralillo group under the command of Edilio Díaz Crespo operated in the region of Colón. As it developed, it was restructured into two detachments, Mario Muñoz and René Fraga, and operated in Colón and Cárdenas under the command of Edilio Díaz and Lázaro Blanco. The group from Agramonte was reorganized and joined the Luis Avila Detachment. In the last part of December, two PSP groups began to form. The Enrique Hart, Mario Muñoz, and René Fraga Moreno Detachments were organized into a single unit, the Enrique Hart Column, in December 1958.

6

Toward January 1, 1959

The failure of the April general strike was due to several factors, most notably the uncertain implementation of methods of struggle that were later replaced by surprise attacks characteristic of urban commando military actions and guerrilla hit-and-run operations. The absence of Frank País, the most skilled leader of the underground civilian structure and the architect of the plan for the general strike, further hindered the implementation of the plan. The April setback altered the civil-military balance within the revolutionary movement and facilitated the ascendancy of the military. The national leadership of the MR 26-7 became centralized under the direction of Fidel Castro as commander in chief of the rebel army even as the MR 26-7 militia and the political command became more military oriented. The MR 26-7, as a party giving form to a consolidated underground under a decentralized command in provinces, regions, and municipalities, with a powerful network all over the island, was converted into a structure of civil-military support for the rebel army.

The civic resistance made up of professionals, businesspeople, fraternal associations, religious organizations, and the patriotic sectors of the bourgeoisie began to collapse in December 1958. But in the provinces of Havana and Matanzas the MRC persisted as a stronghold of the guerrilla logistical rearguard, especially for the newly formed Angel Almeijeiras guerrilla column. As a result of its short-lived existence, the National Student Front planned very few actions; one of the most notable was the preparation for the April strike. The insurrectional workers' movement continued to evolve and prepare for the workers' congress in arms in the Sierra Maestra that convened in October. The sugar workers' conference that took

place on the northern front of Las Villas in December 1958 was organized in the western part of the island.

The deterioration of the civic resistance precipitated the
breakup of the main sectors of the patriotic revolutionary social
movement: workers, students, and the middle strata consisting of
the patriotic bourgeoisie jointly acting with fraternal, religious, and
civic organizations.[1] These three large forces, structured as the
workers' section, the FEN, and the MRC, represented the principal
social support base of the MR 26-7 and its program.

At a meeting at Altos de Mompié in the Sierra Maestra, Fidel
Castro asked for an analysis of the methods used and the mistakes
made in the April 9 strike. All members of the national leadership
attended, with Ernesto (Ché) Guevara present as guest. Reports
were delivered by Faustino Pérez, coordinator of Havana and
leader of strike preparations in the capital; Marcelo Fernández
Font, national coordinator; David Salvador, national workers' coordinator, who had recently replaced insurgent trade union leader
Antonio Torres; and Commander Daniel, national chief of the militia.[2]

After a review of the flaws in the preparation and direction of
the strike, the MR 26-7 leadership determined to change politico-
military strategy and reorganize and restructure the national leadership accordingly. Henceforth military and political structures were
consolidated under Castro as chief of all military forces and secretary-general of the MR 26-7. The political sector of the national leadership relocated to the Sierra Maestra and reorganized as a five-
member national executive committee subordinate to Castro.
Haydée Santamaría was appointed delegate of the movement
abroad, charged with responsibility for the acquisition of weapons
for the rebel army. Santamaría took up residence in Miami and replaced Raúl Chibás as treasurer. Chibás went to the Sierra Maestra
to coordinate contacts between the Sierra leadership and the civic
resistance. Luis Busch was appointed to head July 26 sections in the
United States, Central America, and South America. Marcelo Fernández continued as MR 26-7 coordinator of the underground structure. Antonio Torres served in the national workers' delegation, operating out of the Frank País Second Front, charged with
implementing the agreement of expanding the work of FON and in-
tegrating the National United Workers' Front (Frente Obrero Nacional Unido; FONU) and the workers' sections of the opposition
organizations and parties.[3] Comandante Delio Gómez Ochoa, second in command of the José Martí Column One, was appointed action

delegate of western headquarters and relocated to Havana. Carlos Franqui was appointed national propaganda chief, in charge of Radio Rebelde in the Sierra Maestra. All were subordinate to Castro.

A commander of the Sierra rather than the militia was appointed because of disagreement within the leadership regarding hit-and-run actions. These actions were to become generalized all over the country, and for that reason all activities of the underground were to be subordinated to the national action delegate in support of the guerrilla units and armed commandos, to again begin preparing the revolutionary environment necessary for a subsequent general strike. Once conditions were ready, the guerrillas would move from east to west in a coordinated offensive against the regime, consolidating all power in the MR 26-7 rebel army backed by the revolutionary general strike.

The Civic Resistance Movement all but disappeared after the failed April strike. Although it was not formally dissolved in Havana and Matanzas, where it remained strong and active, a new July 26 structure known as the Base Revolutionary Cells (Celulas Revolucionarias de Base; CRB) was set up as counterpart in the provincial capitals; its coordinators were appointed provincial leaders. Organized by members of the MR 26-7, the CRB established a network of supporters that offered safehouses and resources for the underground structure. A supply front was also created at a national level and located in Havana. Together the CRB and the supply front were to perform the tasks previously assigned the civic resistance once the war generalized to all provinces. The MRC was to operate principally as a logistical support network in the capital and Havana and Matanzas Provinces.[4]

Comandante Gómez Ochoa, as national delegate of the MR 26-7 in action-related matters, was charged with opening new combat fronts. He began in Pinar del Río by establishing a zone of operations in the Sierra de los Organos under the leadership of Comandante Dermidio Escalona. During his stay in Havana between May and October 1958, Gómez Ochoa also prepared conditions for another front in the hills of Madruga, backed mainly by Bejucal's MR 26-7 municipal leadership. Several months later Castro requested Gómez Ochoa to return to the Sierra Maestra. He was replaced as chief of the western provinces by Comandante Diego Paneque, who organized Havana's front and the guerrilla unit of Matanzas. They would be organized as the Angel Almeijeiras Column and Enrique Hart Column in Madruga and Matanzas, respectively.[5]

In August the Matanzas provincial leadership was reorganized, and included Francisco Chavarry (coordinator), Manuel Yepe (head of propaganda), Felipe Quintana (action chief), and Verena Pino Machado (finances). Later Eugenio Cabrera, who had operated as head of the workers' section and FON in Colón, was promoted as provincial workers' coordinator. At the same time, Ibrahim de la Cruz became provincial supplies chief.[6]

The new provincial leadership faced a critical situation in Matanzas. Provincial and regional leaderships had been shattered in the repressive wave that followed the failed strike. From July to August, its underground and guerrilla structures had lost contact with the national leadership. Most of the provincial leaders had been captured or sent to other provinces or emigrated abroad. During this period the provincial coordinator and the regional coordinator in Cárdenas eventually contacted two of the network's liaisons and reestablished contacts in the regions of guerrilla operations.

During this same period, some of the most important rebel groups disappeared, including those of La Paciencia, Santa Ana-Cidra, Las Piedras, Bolondrón, Pedro Betancourt, and some of the Chiva Muerta groups, especially Jovellanos, some of whom left for the Pinar del Río front or the Escambray. The group that Esteban Hernández tried to organize in the Sierra de Bibanasí did not materialize. Most of the urban and rural commandos organized for the April strike, however, remained in their territories in Colón, Cárdenas, the Las Villas–Matanzas border, Jovellanos, and the Matanzas-Madruga border.

Despite increased repression and terror and the subsequent imprisonment and death of combatants, fighters who had not been forced to leave their areas of residence or lacked the resources to do so remained active on their own, listening to messages from the national leadership in broadcasts from Radio Rebelde. The rebel groups continued to evolve as nuclei of the guerrilla army and set up support bases in their respective regions. In September the new military leadership of Matanzas Province visited rural areas where these groups operated to promote the organization of the detachments and platoons that would make up the Havana-Matanzas front.

The command of both provinces was divided into two separate units. The politico-military command of the MR 26-7 drew a perpendicular line from the city of Matanzas to the south; guerrilla forces were to operate throughout the territory, including the plains of Colón. Both commands settled in the Madruga-Matanzas heights and led the platoons of the Angel Almeijeiras column, led by Captain

José Garcerán del Vals, and the Enrique Hart column, led by Juan Ramón López Fleites. Garcerán had been trained in a Mexican camp and landed with a shipment of weapons at Punta Hicacos in the mangroves of the Dupont area in Varadero. The main purpose of the two platoons was to distract the armed forces with operations along the north of both provinces, while the invading Antonio Maceo Column One led by Comandante Camilo Cienfuegos moved west.

Felipe Quintana and Juan Ramón López Fleites prepared the Matanzas plan of action for urban zones and the guerrilla plans for rural areas. López Fleites visited each guerrilla group, beginning with units in the Valle de Guamacaro. He strengthened their military training by applying the methods used in the Sierra Maestra; once they had begun hit-and-run operations, he moved on. Meanwhile, local leaders traveled to Yaguajay's northern front to meet with Cienfuegos, informing him of the organizing activities and areas where guerrilla groups operated in Madruga and Matanzas and the means available to support the invading column to Pinar del Río.[7]

$$* \quad * \quad *$$

The final clashes between the rebel army and government armed forces and the defeat of the latter during the offensive and counteroffensive in 1958 produced a gradual breakdown and demoralization of government forces and the eventual surrender of entire garrisons without a fight. In the early hours of January 1, 1959, Batista informed his closest collaborators that he was fleeing the country.[8] Batista told his associates that "forced by landowners, colonos, and church authorities" and in a situation in which the troops were not winning "one single skirmish, with weakened commands and battalions surrendering to the enemy without fighting," he had decided to appoint General Eulogio Cantillo to establish a military junta. He tendered his resignation and accepted the resignations of Anselmo Alliegro, José Rodríguez Calderón, Pedro Rodríguez Avila, Luis Robaina Piedra, Francisco Tabernilla Palmero, Roberto Fernández Miranda, Juan Rojas González, and Pilar García.[9]

Throughout December a military conspiracy against Batista had developed in the Matanzas regiment, led by General Carlos Cantillo, brother of Eulogio, in discussion with the MR 26-7 provincial leadership. Since the beginning of the armed struggle in

1956, the MR 26-7 had rejected a military junta as a solution to the political crisis. This position was ratified in the April 9 manifestos and repeatedly stressed by Castro even before negotiations with Eulogio Cantillo began. In Matanzas Province officers linked to the high-level military led by Eulogio Cantillo and his brother Carlos attempted to reach an understanding with the provincial underground leadership in December 1958.

Another conspiracy joined with Eulogio Cantillo. In Las Villas Colonel Florentino Rosell Leyva, commander of a train convoy, agreed with General Río Chaviano, the military chief of Las Villas, on a plan for a coup d'état. Rosell established contact with Cantillo, requesting his support to arrange to cooperate with MR 26-7 chiefs, with Castro's personal consent.[10] Cantillo agreed to support the conspiracy and incorporate his brother Carlos, of Matanzas, Colonel José Rego Rubido, chief of the Santiago de Cuba regiment, and Commodore Manuel Camero, head of the Oriente naval district. He then sent a message to Castro informing him of the conspiracy and the proposed conditions. On December 22 Castro responded by rejecting all conditions and demanding the unconditional surrender of the armed forces to the rebel army.[11]

In fact, by December 1958 military units and police forces across the island had ceased operation. Many deserted and fled. Some joined the insurrectionary forces. Entire units were quartered at their posts waiting for orders that never arrived. In the Oriente countryside, many towns were in rebel hands; Santiago de Cuba, Bayamo, and Holguín were seriously threatened. The Camagüey regiment was on the defensive. In Las Villas many towns had fallen into insurgent hands after most government soldiers had laid down their arms. Under the circumstances Havana was becoming increasingly isolated. The main railway transportation bridges had been destroyed, and road transportation was practically paralyzed. Fuel supplies were disappearing.[12]

These were the days of the most intense initiatives of the rebel army. On December 30 Castro ordered his troops to march on Santiago de Cuba. He then ordered Che Guevara, as military chief of Las Villas, not to accept the truce but rather to collect all weapons and distribute them to MR 26-7 members. He was to march with the Ciro Redondo Column to Santa Clara, while Cienfuegos attacked the Yaguajay garrison with the Antonio Maceo Column.[13] These actions dealt the coup de grace to the regime, forcing Batista to accelerate plans to flee.

Castro called a meeting of the national leadership at La Rinconada in Sierra Maestra; MR 26-7 provincial coordinators attended. The coordinator of Matanzas, Francisco Chavarry, returned to the province on December 31 with instructions to establish communications with the local military. During his absence, Manuel Yepe had made initial contact with the bishop of Matanzas, asking the bishop to intervene on behalf of Verena Pina, the imprisoned provincial head of finances.[14]

The meeting between the bishop and the chief of the regiment occurred in the Matanzas cathedral. It was at this point the local MR 26-7 leaders learned from the bishop that a group of officers wanted to establish contact with the MR 26-7. Several days earlier Felipe Quintana had met with a lieutenant of the Cidra army unit, through OA operative Pepe Lima, who collaborated with MR 26-7. The agreement called for an operation simulating an attack on Cidra, whereupon the lieutenant would surrender the garrison to rebel forces.[15]

On January 1 Yepe and Quintana made an early tour of the city. They met with Chavarry, relayed instructions agreed upon in the Sierra Maestra enjoining the provincial leadership to demand "full power to July 26" and "Urrutia for president." Both slogans represented a radical position rejecting pacts with anyone: no civic institution, no military junta, no provisional government. There was to be no coalition—with the DR, the PSP, the OA, or any other civic organization.

After their meeting, Chavarry, Yepe, and Quintana proceeded to the regiment. The bishop accompanied Chavarry and Yepe to the office of the regimental chief, while the provincial action head, Quintana, and Onanay, municipal coordinator of Matanzas, met with the chief of police, Salas Cañizares. The leaders of the MR 26-7 upheld the Sierra agreements. Army chiefs were to concentrate their troops from all garrisons, posts, and police stations at the regimental command and wait for another meeting with Cienfuegos, the head of the rebel army, whereupon they were to relinquish political power of the province.

The negotiations were successful. While the meeting was taking place, the high military command had learned that the people's sectors had already taken to the streets, the MR 26-7 militia had taken over the police station, and guerrilla troops in Matanzas had seized San Miguel de los Baños. The MR 26-7 leaders in the headquarters of the Matanzas regiment convinced the army that rebel operations had extended across the entire island and only the MR 26-7 was capable of restoring order. To avoid further bloodshed and looting, the army ceded power to the rebels.

For the MR 26-7 leadership, the essential issue was not surrender of the army but the concentration of their military forces in the regiment in order to seize political power immediately upon Batista's flight. They rejected outright the prospect of the military junta, especially since the guerrilla army and the militia of Matanzas were ready to attack and take over garrisons. On January 1, 1959, nearly the entire province was in the hands of the MR 26-7.

Once the negotiations had ended, the provincial leaders raised the July 26 banner in the streets; the time had come to call for the political general strike. The civilian leadership led by Chavarry turned city hall into the July 26 headquarters. Roberto Yepe and Hector Rodríguez Llompart occupied Radio Matanzas and broadcast instructions for the general strike. They also ordered the mass production of black and red armbands, which they distributed throughout the province as the symbol of the revolution. At the same time, the military leadership led by Quintana convened the MR 26-7 underground structure that organized brigades and militia.

* * *

Cienfuegos arrived in Matanzas on January 2 with Commanders William Gálvez and Victor Bordón. The head of the Enrique Hart Column, López Fleites, joined him, together with Oscar Gutiérrez Barceló and a group from his detachment. General Carlos Cantillo welcomed them all in his office. Cantillo inquired about who would assume command of the regiment; Cienfuegos appointed Gálvez.

Cantillo called the several thousand troops of regimental command to the military square, where the official surrender of Matanzas regiment to the MR 26-7 took place. "We have unconditionally surrendered," Cantillo proclaimed. "All soldiers must turn over their weapons. Comandante Camilo Cienfuegos has been generous enough to allow all officers to keep their pistols."[16] Later that afternoon Cienfuegos went on to Camp Columbia in Havana, where General Eulogio Cantillo and the officers of the military junta, including Ramón Barquín, turned over the command to him.

Several days later Castro arrived in Matanzas after stopping in Colón to visit the home of Mario Muñoz Monroy, member of the first national leadership of the movement and the first martyr of the attack on Moncada. Marcelo Fernández, national coordinator from Cárdenas, preceded him, convening the provincial leaders in the city hall, where they welcomed Castro a few hours later. Afterward Castro spoke to the people who had gathered in Libertad Park.

* * *

On January 3 the revolutionary government held the first meeting of the Council of Ministers at the University of Oriente. Castro was appointed commander in chief, a position that constitutionally corresponded to the president of the republic; the new president and the council decided that Castro was obliged to take that position as leader of the revolution. The members of the revolutionary government arrived in Havana by airplane on January 5; they were welcomed by Cienfuegos.

Cuba had won its national liberation and independence under the leadership of the MR 26-7. The forces of the revolution were represented in a structure that had unified social groups, civic associations, and religious organizations. The MR 26-7 program represented the laws and reforms historically demanded by Cubans, who called for the establishment of a republic of justice dedicated to economic reconstruction and, with it, the struggle for Cuban self-determination and economic sovereignty.

Acronyms

BRAC	Bureau to Repress Communist Activities (Buró de Represión a las Actividades Comunistas)
CRB	Base Revolutionary Cells (Celulas Revolucionarias de Base)
CTC	Confederation of Cuban Workers (Confederación de Trabajadores Cubanos)
DEU	Directorate of University Students (Directorio Estudiantil Universitario)
DR	Revolutionary Directorate (Directorio Revolucionario)
FEIC	Student Federation of the Cárdenas Institute (Federación Estudiantil del Instituto de Cárdenas)
FEIM	Student Federation of the Institute of Matanzas (Federación Estudiantil del Instituto de Matanzas)
FEN	National Students' Front (Frente Estudiantil Nacional)
FEU	University Student Federation (Federación Estudiantil Universitaria)
FNTA	National Federation of Sugar Workers (Federación Nacional de Trabajadores Azucareros)
FNTT	National Federation of Textile Workers (Federación Nacional de Trabajadores Textiles)
FOMN	National Maritime Workers' Federation (Federación Obrera Marítima Nacional)
FON	National Workers' Front (Frente Obrero Nacional)
FONU	National United Workers' Front (Frente Obrero Nacional Unido)
FPTT	Provincial Federation of Textile Workers (Federación Provincial de Trabajadores Textileras)
ICEA	Cuban Sugar Stabilization Institute (Instituto Cubano de Estabilización del Azucár)

MNR	National Revolutionary Movement (Movimiento Nacionalista Revolucionario)
MR 26-7	July 26 Revolutionary Movement (Movimiento Revolucionario 26 Julio)
MRC	Civic Resistance Movement (Movimiento Resistencia Cívica)
OA	Auténtico Party Organization (Organización Auténtico)
OAS	Organization of American States
ORIT	Inter-American Regional Organization of Workers (Organización Regional Interamericana de Trabajadores)
PPC(O)	Cuban People's Party (Orthodox) (Partido del Pueblo Cubano [Ortodoxo])
PSP	Popular Socialist Party (Partido Socialista Popular)
SAR	Society of Friends of the Republic (Sociedad de Amigos de la República)
SIM	Military Intelligence Service (Servicio de Inteligencia Militar)

Chronology

1952

March 10   Fulgencio Batista seizes power through a military coup in Havana. Colonel Eduardo Martín, chief of the Plácido Regiment in Matanzas, refuses to relinquish command pending instruction from President Carlos Prío Socarrás. By night fall President Prío has taken asylum and Colonel Martín is arrested.

March 12   FEIM issues a manifesto condemning the military coup.

April 2   Federation of University Students (FEU) summons students, workers, and the population at large to participate in a "Wake for the Constitution" to be held at the University of Havana.

May 20   Rafael García Bárcena organizes the Movimiento Nacionalista Revolucionario (MNR).

Nov. 27   FEIM calls for a demonstration to condemn the coup at the birth home of Carlos Verdugo, one of the students executed by Spain in 1871.

Dec. 7   On the occasion of the commemoration of the death of Antonio Maceo, the FEU, FEIM, and other citizens of Matanzas organize a protest march to denounce the Batista dictatorship.

1953

March 10   Anti-government student protests are organized in Havana and Matanzas.

April 5   A MNR conspiracy against the government is uncovered and the principal leaders are arrested.

May 8   The FEIM and the union of La Rayonera factory commemorate the death of Antonio Guiteras at El Morrillo in Matanzas. Participants subsequently are detained and imprisoned.

July 26   Fidel Castro and others attack the military barracks in Santiago
           de Cuba and at Bayamo.
Sept. 23   Trial of Fidel Castro begins. In Havana, the police mount a raid
           against the University of Havana.

1954

Jan. 9   Strikes in the henequen plantations and factories paralyze pro-
           duction in Matanzas, Cárdenas, and Limonar.
May 21   Government adopts repressive measures against factory and
           field workers, including detentions and arrests.

1955

May 15   Fidel Castro and other participants in the Moncada barracks as-
           sault are released from prison.
May 17   Fidel Castro and student leader José Antonio Echeverría meet in
           Havana.
June 9   The National Federation of Sugar Workers (FNTA) in Matanzas
           present Fidel Castro a check to support the struggle against the
           Batista government. Castro appoints Jaime López as provincial
           delegate of the 26 July Movement in Matanzas.
July 7   Fidel Castro leaves for Mexico to organize opposition from
           abroad.
Sept. 12   Workers of the henequen plantations in Cárdenas undertake
           spontaneous sabotage acts.
Nov.   Month-long student demonstrations erupt across the island, in
           Santiago de Cuba, Matanzas, Artemisa, Santa Clara, Camagüey,
           Holguín, and Havana.

1956

Feb. 24   José Antonio Echeverría announces the creation of the Directo-
           rio Revolucionario under the auspices of the FEU.
April 29   Elements of the Auténtico party attack the Goicuría military bar-
           racks in Matanzas.
Aug. 30   The Pact of Mexico is reached between the MR 26-7 and the
           FEU.
Nov. 30   Uprisings across the island coincide with the return of Fidel
           Castro.
Dec. 2   Fidel Castro lands in Oriente province.

1957

March 13	José Antonio Echeverría is slain in an abortive assault against the presidential palace.
July	The Civic Resistance Movement of the MR 26-7 is established.
July 30	Frank País, the national coordinator of MR 26-7, is killed.
Sept. 25	Naval uprising occurs in Cienfuegos.
Nov.	Campaign against sugar production is inaugurated.

1958

Jan.	Guerrilla units launch operations in Matanzas.
April 9	Abortive general strike is called by the MR 26-7.
August	Rebel Army in the Sierra Maestra mounts counteroffensive with the organization of two columns to carry the war into the western provinces.
Dec. 17	Battle of Santa Clara signals the end of the Batista government.

1959

Jan. 1	Batista flees the island.
Jan. 8	Fidel Castro reaches Havana.

Notes

Chapter One

1. Fondo Tribunal de Urgencia, Legajo 152, 1952, Archivo Provincial Histórico de Matanzas (hereinafter cited as APHM). Interview in 1983 with Ricardo González Trejo and Manuel del Cueto, founders and coordinators of MR 26-7 in Jovellanos and Cárdenas, respectively; Oscar Gutiérrez Barceló, member of the action and sabotage brigade; Israel, Dolores, and Antonio Gil Perdomo, originally members of the Auténtico Party and later part of the action and sabotage brigade in El Cocal and El Bolo in Matanzas; Emérito García, president of the Agrupación Campesina Ortodoxo of Jagüey Grande and later chief of the MR 26-7 guerrilla unit Luis Avila operating in southern Matanzas.

2. Fondo Partido del Pueblo Cubano Ortodoxo, "Programa," Archivo Nacional de Cuba, Havana (hereinafter cited as ANC). Louis A. Pérez Jr., *Army Politics in Cuba, 1898–1958* (Pittsburgh, 1976), pp. 125–127; Hugh Thomas, *Cuba, la lucha por la libertad* (Barcelona, 1974), p. 1009.

3. "Editorial" and "En Cuba," *Bohemia,* 44 (March 16, 1952), pp. 64–65; Rafael Estenger, "La doble cara del golpe de estado," *Bohemia,* 44 (March 16, 1952), p. 49; Pedro Barrera Pérez, "Por qué el ejército no derrotó a Castro," *Bohemia Libre* (Caracas), 53 (July 16, 1961), p. 78.

4. Barrera Pérez, "Por qué el ejército no derrotó a Castro," p. 78; Pérez, *Army Politics in Cuba,* pp. 127, 131.

5. Thomas, *Cuba, la lucha por la libertad,* pp. 1008–1012; Francis L. McCarthy, "Historia de una revolución," *Bohemia,* 44 (March 30, 1952), pp. 66–68.

6. Pérez, *Army Politics in Cuba,* pp. 126–127; McCarthy, "Historia de una revolución," pp. 66–68.

7. Thomas, *Cuba, la lucha por la libertad,* p. 1011; Barrera Pérez, "Por qué el ejército no derrotó a Castro," p. 78.

8. Javier Barahana, "El 10 de marzo en La Habana," *Carteles,* 33 (March 16, 1952), p. 52.

9. "En Cuba," *Bohemia,* 44 (March 9, 1952), p. 59.

10. Ibid. (March 16, 1952), p. 62; Estenger, "La doble cara del golpe," p. 49.

11. Antonio Llano Montes, "El velorio de la Constitución en la Universidad," *Carteles,* 33 (April 13, 1952), p. 37; *Bohemia,* 44 (March 23, 1952), p. 53.

12. Interviews with Manuel del Cueto, Víctor Guerra, Cárdenas, 1984; Emérito García, Jagüey Grande, 1983. Documents of Mario Muñoz Monroy in possession of Natalia Revuelta.

13. *Bohemia,* 44 (March 30, 1952), p. 54.

14. Ibid. (March 16, 1952), p. 63 and (March 23, 1952), sup. 5.

15. "Testimonio de Enrique Borbonet, dirigente del grupo de oficiales que conspiraron contra Batista," in William Gálvez, *Camilo, señor de la vanguardia* (Havana, 1979), pp. 433–434; Andrés Valdespino, "¿Culpables de que?" *Bohemia,* 58 (April 22, 1956), pp. 55, 92–93; "La conspiración del 3 de abril," *Bohemia,* 48 (April 15, 1956), pp. 63–70, 72–76; Enrique Gutiérrez, "La conspiración para la rebelión militar," *Carteles,* 37 (April 15, 1956), pp. 38–40.

16. Interviews with Amador del Valle, chief of action of the MR 26-7 in Cárdenas, and Leandro Marín, MR 26-7 coordinator in the municipality of Martí, 1985; Vicente Cubillas, "Cienfuegos: un pueblo a la vanguardia de la revolución," *Bohemia,* 57 (September 3, 1965), pp. 31–39; Aldo Menéndez, "Un levantamiento popular," *Bohemia,* 65 (September 7, 1973), pp. 4–11; Faustino Pérez, "Antecedentes del alzamiento de Cienfuegos," *Granma,* September 4, 1971, p. 2.

17. Rodolfo Villamil, "Por qué me uní a las fuerzas de Fidel Castro," *Bohemia,* 51 (March 8, 1959), pp. 40–41, 114.

18. Intereviews with Edilio Díaz Crespo, Havana, 1972, 1980; Francisco Díaz Fontela, Colón, 1984; Ciro Díaz Mingas, Los Arabos, 1986; Rubén Blanco, coordinator of the MR 26-7 in Colón.

19. Earl E. T. Smith to Secretary of State, December 2, 1958, in Department of State, *Foreign Relations of the United States, 1958–1950: Cuba* (Washington, D.C., 1991), pp. 276–277.

20. Consejo de Ministro, "Ley Constitucional," April 4, 1952, Fondo Presidencia, ANC.

Chapter Two

1. See "Congresos de Historia de Cuba," Instituto de Literatura y Lingüistica, Academia de Ciencias, Havana (hereinafter cited as ILL).

2. Misión Truslow, "Informe," ANC.

3. See Emilio Roig de Leuchsenring, "Discurso de apertura," Congreso Nacional de Historiadores, Jiguaní, 1956, ILL.

4. Raúl Roa, *La revolución se fue a bolina* (Havana, 1976), pp. 15–16.

5. Ibid., pp. 11–13.
6. See Julio Vicente González, *La reforma universitaria* (Buenos Aires, 1925).
7. Berta Alonso, "La participación de los jóvenes del actual municipio de Centro Habana en los sucesos del 26 de Julio" (manuscript, n.d., copy in author's possession).
8. Interviews with Ricardo González Trejo; Manuel del Cueto; Oscar Gutiérrez Barceló; Víctor Guerra, member of the Ortodoxo youth and later a founder of the MR 26-7 in Cárdenas; Emérito García; Israel Gil Perdomo; Eugenio Cabrera, MR 26-7 regional coordinator of the labor sector of Colón; Lázaro Blanco, sugar workers' leader and chief of the unit René Fraga Moreno; Edilio Díaz Crespo, chief of the MR 26-7 guerrilla unit Mario Muñoz.
9. *El Mundo*, December 24, 1955. Ricardo Alarcón, "Los estudiantes y la lucha contra Batista," *OCLAE* 2 (May 1968), pp. 16–19; Javier Rodríguez, "José Antonio Echeverría y la clase obrera," *Bohemia*, 59 (March 10, 1967), pp. 52–55; José Antonio Echeverría, "Constitución del Directorio Revolucionario: discurso de José Antonio Echeverría, Febrero 24 de 1954," in Organización de Bibliotecas Ambulantes, *13 documents de la insurrección* (Havana, 1959), pp. 31–34.
10. *Bohemia*, 44 (March 16, 1952), p. 18 and (March 23, 1952), p. 54. Broadsides "Pueblo" and "Manifiestos," signed by the Directorio Juvenil de Matanzas, March 20, 1952. Copies in APHM.
11. Jules Dubois, *Fidel Castro: Biografía* (Mexico, 1959), p. 27.
12. *Bohemia*, 44 (March 23, 1952), sup. 4, 16; Faure Chomón, "El movimiento estudiantil: foco insurreccional," *Alma Mater*, 136 (November 1972), pp. 34–35.
13. Fondo Tribunal de Urgencia, Legajo 147, Case 558, July 17, 1952, ANC.
14. José Leyva, "Apuntes para los asaltos a los cuarteles Moncada y de Bayamo" (manuscript, 1982, copy in author's possession); Juan Grillo Hernández, *Biografía de Mario Muñoz* (Havana, 1982), pp. 14, 17, 20–23, 25–27.
15. Fondo Tribunal de Urgencia, Legajo 130, APHM, including the cases of Angel Díaz, Andrés Rodríguez Fraga, and Julio and Rafael Fuente.
16. Ibid.
17. Ibid.
18. *Bohemia*, 45 (January 25, 1953), p. 59 and (February 22, 1953), p. 43. Interview with Basilio Rodríguez, Havana, 1986.
19. *El Imparcial* (Matanzas), July 28, 1953.
20. *Carteles*, 33 (April 13, 1952), p. 15; Thomas, *Cuba, la lucha por la libertad*, pp. 1029–1038; *El Imparcial*, September 19 and 22, 1953; October 30, 1953; *Bohemia*, 45 (March 15, 1953), sup. 60, 67; *El Mundo*, September 24, 1953; Marta Rojas, *La Generación del Centenario en el juicio del Moncada* (Havana, 1965), pp. 29–73.

21. Fondo Tribunal de Urgencia, Legajos 135–139, APHM; *El Imparcial,* March 23 and 26, 1953; April 8, 1953; July 27 and 28, 1953; September 24, 1953.

22. Juan Nuiry Sánchez, *Presente: Apuntes para la historia del movimiento estudiantil cubano* (Havana, 1988), pp. 146–147; *Información,* April 20, 1955, and November 14, 1956; Juan Nuiry Sánchez, "José Antonio Echeverría, pensamiento y acción," *Bohemia,* 59 (March 10, 1967), pp. 74–78; Javier Rodríguez, "Visión de José Antonio Echeverría," *Bohemia,* 60 (March 8, 1968), pp. 50–57.

23. *El Mundo,* May 22, 1955.

24. *El Mundo,* June 16 and 22, 1955; July 10 and 16, 1955; Enrique Rodríguez Loeches, "8 de mayo de 1955: homenaje de Echeverría a Guiteras," *Bohemia,* 62 (May 8, 1970), pp. 12–15.

25. *El Mundo,* July 10, 1955; Nuiry Sánchez, *Presente,* pp. 113, 261.

26. Fidel Castro, "Mensaje al Congreso del PPC(O)" and "Manifiesto No. 1 del MR 26-7," August 1955, Fondo Especial, ANC.

27. *El Mundo,* November 20 and 30, 1955.

28. Ibid., December 1, 2, 3, 4, and 6, 1955.

29. Ibid., December 7, 1955; Reinaldo Peñalver Moral, "Noviembre–Diciembre de 1955: 3 días de violencia estudiantil," *Bohemia,* 65 (November 23, 1973), pp. 103–105.

30. *El Mundo,* December 14 and 15, 1955; Javier Gutiérrez, "El dramático viernes de la semana pasada," *Carteles,* 36 (December 11, 1955), pp. 46–47.

31. *Carteles,* 37 (January 1, 1956), p. 18; Nuiry Sánchez, *Presente,* p. 14.

32. *Bohemia,* 48 (January 1, 1956), sup. 16 and (February 5, 1956), p. 47.

33. Ibid. (February 26, 1956), p. 61.

34. Nuiry Sánchez, *Presente,* pp. 147–148; Jaime Suchlicki, "El estudiantado de la Universidad de La Habana en la política cubana, 1956–1957," *Journal of Inter-American Studies,* 9 (January 1967), pp. 145–167; Fidel Castro, "Declaración desde México," *Bohemia,* 48 (July 1, 1956), p. 62.

35. "El Pacto de México (M 7-26 y DR), Septiembre de 1956," in Organización de Bibliotecas Ambulantes y Populares, *13 documentos de la insurrección* (Havana, 1959), pp. 35–39.

36. Nuiry Sánchez, *Presente,* p. 148.

Chapter Three

1. Pelayo Cuervo, "Efectos de la política capitalista en la economía rural de Cuba," *Bohemia,* 44 (December 7, 1952), p. 17; Carlos Franqui, "Los problemas obreros," *Carteles,* 37 (January 8, 1956), pp. 38–39.

2. *El Imparcial,* July 23, 1953; *Bohemia,* 44 (September 28, 1952), pp. 78, 82, and (October 5, 1952), p. 72.

3. *El Mundo*, September 8, 1953.

4. *El Imparcial*, February 23, 1954; March 2, 5, 10, and 25, 1954.

5. Ibid., October 17, 1953; February 24, 1954; March 2 and 5, 1954; April 20 and 25, 1954.

6. *Prensa Libre*, January 6, 1954.

7. Ibid., January 9, 1954.

8. Ibid., January 19, 1954.

9. Ibid., January 29, 1954.

10. Ibid., February 3, 1954.

11. *Bohemia*, 46 (February 28, 1954), p. 31.

12. *Bohemia*, 46 (April 18, 1954), pp. 70–71.

13. César García del Pino, "Cronología" (manuscript, n.d., Biblioteca Nacional José Martí), p. 36; *Bohemia*, 46 (May 16, 1954), p. 19.

14. *Bohemia*, 46 (May 23, 1954), p. 71.

15. Ibid., (November 21, 1954), pp. 62–65.

16. *El Mundo*, February 8 and 9, 1955.

17. Ibid., January 21 and 26, 1955.

18. Ibid., February 1, 1955.

19. Ibid., February 9, 1955.

20. Ibid., February 20, 1955.

21. Ibid., March 17, 1955.

22. Ibid., May 4, 1955.

23. Ibid., June 11, 12, and 15, 1955.

24. Ibid., June 19 and 21, 1955, and July 2, 1955. Interviews with Edilio Díaz Crespo, Havana, 1982, and Eugenio Cabrera, Matanzas, 1996.

25. Ibid., June 26 and 17, 1955, and July 10 and 28, 1955.

26. Ibid., July 8, 1955.

27. García del Pino, "Cronología," p. 52; *Bohemia*, 45 (December 26, 1953), pp. 73–74.

28. *El Mundo*, June 2, 1955.

29. "Cartas a Alejandro [Fidel Castro]," Oficina de Publicaciones de Asunto Históricos, Consejo de Estado, Havana.

30. *El Imparcial*, October 17, 1953; *Bohemia*, 44 (October 5, 1952), p. 25; "Expedientes de Jesús Soto," 1952, 1953, Fondo Tribunal de Urgencia, Legajo 160, 1953, APHM.

31. *El Imparcial*, January 10, 11, and 20, 1954.

32. Ibid., December 2, 1953; January 11, 1954; and March 7, 8, and 24, 1954.

33. *Bohemia*, 46 (May 16, 1954), p. 56.

34. *El Imparcial*, May 4, 7, 8, 12, and 21, 1954; June 24, 1954; *Bohemia*, 46 (May 1, 1954), p. 20.

35. *El Imparcial*, June 24, 1954.

36. Ibid., June 24, 28, and 29, 1954; and July 29, 1954.

37. Ibid., August 26, 1955.

38. Ibid., September 2 and 12, 1955; *El Mundo*, September 14, 1955.

39. *El Imparcial,* October 4, 28, 22, 23, and 27, 1955; November 16, 17, and 29, 1955; December 22 and 23, 1955; *El Mundo,* October 21, 1955.
40. *El Imparcial,* December 22 and 23, 1955.
41. Ibid., January 5 and 21, 1956.
42. Ibid., March 9, 1957.
43. Ibid., May 3, 1957.
44. Ibid., January 20 and 22, 1958; February 15, 1958.
45. Ibid., April 24, 1958, and May 10, 1958.
46. Ibid., July 17, 1958.
47. Ibid., July 6, 1953.
48. Ibid., January 14, 1955, and February 3 and 6, 1954.
49. Ibid., October 26, 1956.
50. Ibid., October 31, 1955.
51. Ibid., May 17, 18, and 22, 1955.
52. *El Mundo,* September 8 and 10, 1955.
53. *El Imparcial,* January 7, 23, and 29, 1958.
54. Fondo Tribunal de Urgencia, Legajos 136–140, APHM, which contain eighty-seven cases of cane burnings during the year 1953, principally in Limonar, Coliseo, San Miguel de los Baños, Guamacaro, Jovellanos, Jagüey Grande, Colón, Ceiba Mocha, and Bolondrón.
55. *El Imparcial,* July 30, 1953, and August 10, 1953. Interview with Manuel de Cueto, Cárdenas, 1984.
56. *El Imparcial,* October 17, 1953.
57. Ibid., February 27, 1954.
58. Ibid., December 12, 1953.
59. Ibid., November 25, 26, and 27, 1954.
60. Ibid., February 22, 1954, and March 1, 1954.
61. Ibid., April 20, 1954.
62. Ibid., December 29, 1954; January 5 and 28, 1955; February 2 and 11, 1955; and March 18, 1955.
63. Ibid., October 5, 1955.
64. Ibid., November 26, 1955.
65. Ibid., December 21, 26, 27, 28, and 29, 1955; *El Mundo,* December 27, 1955.
66. *El Imparcial,* May 23, 1956, and June 12, 1956.
67. Ibid., July 10, 1956.
68. Ibid., June 19 and 20, 1956.
69. Ibid., July 11, 1956, and August 7, 1956.
70. Ibid., July 5, 1956, and September 5 and 27, 1956.
71. Ibid., July 11 and 24, 1956; August 18, 29, and 30, 1956; September 26, 1956; and October 1, 1956.
72. Ibid., December 3 and 26, 1956.
73. Ibid., June 12, 1956.
74. Ibid., April 4, 1957; May 13, 1957; and June 8, 1957.

75. República de Cuba, Ministerio de Defensa Nacional, Ejército, "Informe sobre elementos insurreccionales y actos de sabotaje," June 25, 1957, APHM.
76. *El Imparcial,* June 12, 15, and 22, 1957; July 13, 1957.
77. *El Imparcial,* June 8, 1958.
78. Interview with Lázaro Blanco and Leandro Marín, participants in MR 26-7 guerrilla operations in Cárdenas and Jovellanos, 1986.

Chapter Four

1. Justo Carrillo, *Cuba 1933: Estudiantes, yanquis y soldados* (Santo Domingo, 1985), pp. 263–357.
2. Interviews with Jesús Montané, Melba Hernández, Gabriel Delgado, and Agustín Egurrola Alvarez in Leyva, "Apuntes para los asaltos"; Juan Grillo Hernández, *Biografía de Mario Muñoz* (Havana, 1982), pp. 20, 34–40.
3. Fidel Castro, "Algunos aspectos de la revolución cubana." An interview with Oleg Darushenkov; original transcript in Oficina de Asuntos Históricos, Consejo de Estado de Cuba, Havana.
4. Luis Padilla, "El marxismo-leninismo y la revolución cubana," *Revista Internacional* (Prague), 1 (1979).
5. Leyva, "Apuntes para los asaltos."
6. Fondo Tribunal de Urgencia, Legajo 130, Cases 9, 12, 15, 19, and 29, APHM.
7. Interview with Basilio Rodríguez, director of the FEIM, 1984.
8. Leyva, "Apuntes para los asaltos"; Eduardo Chibás, "El último aldabonzo," August 1951, Fondo Eduardo Chibás, ANC.
9. Leyva, "Apuntes para los asaltos"; Grillo Hernández, *Biografia de Mario Muñoz,* p. 17; *El Imparcial,* July 20, 1953.
10. Fondo Tribunal de Urgencia, Legajo 135, Cases 1–3, 7–9, 11–14, 18–25; Legajo 136, Cases 1–2, 4–26, 28–32, and 52; Legajo 137, Cases 1–2, 4–20, 22–26, 28–30; Legajo 138, Cases 1–14, 17–19, 22–26; Legajo 139, Cases 1–9, 11–25; Legajo 140, Cases 12–13, 22–24, and 26–29, 1956–1958, APHM.
11. Fidel Castro, *La historia me absolverá* (Havana, 1967), pp. 57–70.
12. Padilla, "El marxismo-leninismo y la revolución cubana," pp. 5–7; Fernando Martínez, "La noción de pueblo en 'La historia me absolverá,'" *Verde Olivo,* 15 (November 18, 1973), pp. 26–29.
13. Fondo Tribunal de Urgencia, Legajo 153, 1955, APHM.
14. Interview with Israel Tápanes, a participant in the attack against Moncada, 1985; Israel Tápanes, "Después de Moncada," *Santiago,* 12 (October 1973), pp. 105–126.
15. Interviews with Ricardo González Trejo, Félix Ponce, Juan Manuel, and Cuchi Torres, 1976.

16. Ibid.

17. Ibid.

18. Ibid.

19. Fondo Tribunal de Urgencia, Legago 159, Case 72; Legajos 155 and 156, APHM; Nydia Sarabia, "Santiago esperó el 'Granma,'" *Verde Olivo*, 6 (December 5, 1965), pp. 19–21, 51–52; Juan A. Sánchez Bermúdez, "El treinta de noviembre de 1956 en la historia," *Islas*, 45 (May–August 1973), pp. 131–142.

20. Interviews with Israel Tápanes and Orlando Lima, Havana, 1985 and 1989; Fondo Tribunal de Urgencia, Legajo 155, Cases 8, 9, 21, APHM.

21. Fondo Tribunal de Urgencia, Legajo 152, Case 1; Legajo 153, Cases 12, 22, and 24; Legajo 155, Cases 5, 8–10, 12, 14, 21, and 23; Legajo 156, Cases 7, 8, and 10, APHM.

22. Fidel Castro, "Carta a Carmen Castro," September 17, 1955, in Colectivo de Autoras, *La lección del maestro* (Havana, 1990), pp. 90–100.

23. *El Imparcial,* January 5, 1955; March 28, 1955; May 16, 1957; and January 29, 1958.

24. Interview with Eduardo González Rodríguez, Matanzas, 1976.

25. MR 26-7 Manifiesto, "500 milliones han perdido los obreros! Pueblo al combate por tú revolución!" Fondo Tribunal de Urgencia, Legajo 161, Case 128, 1956, APHM.

26. *El Imparcial,* March 16, 1956; May 22, 1956; June 14, 1956; July 5, 1956; September 12, 1956; October 25 and 29, 1956; and November 11, 1956.

27. Ibid., September 20, 1956; November 6, 1956; Fondo Tribunal de Urgencia, Legajo 157, Cases 6, 11, 13, 24, and 26; Legajo 158, Cases 6 and 20, APHM.

28. Fondo Tribunal de Urgencia, Legajo 159, Case 14, APHM.

29. Ibid., Legajo 157, Cases 6, 11, 13, 24, and 26; Legajo 158, Cases 6 and 10, APHM.

30. *El Imparcial,* November 6, 1956.

31. Interviews with Ricardo González Trejo, Juan Torres, and Félix Ponce, Havana, 1990.

32. Ibid.; Marta Rojas, "Los dias que precedieron a la expedición del Granma," *Bohemia*, 51 (December 27, 1959), pp. 10–13, 139–140.

33. Interviews with Ricardo González Trejo, Juan Torres, and Félix Ponce, Havana, 1990.

34. *El Imparcial,* December 3, 1956.

35. Ibid., December 13, 1956.

36. Ibid., January 5 and 8, 1957; April 26, 1957; and May 17 and 18, 1957.

37. Interview with Ricardo González Trejo, Matanzas, 1976.

38. Fondo Tribunal de Urgencia, Legajo 159, Case 1–3, 6–8, 11, 15–19, 21, 23–25, and 28; Legajo 160, Cases 1, 4, 5, 14, 21, and 23, APHM.

39. Fondo Tribunal de Urgencia, Legajo 157, Cases 6, 11, 13, 24, and 26; Legajo 158, Cases 6 and 10, APHM.

40. Ibid., Legajo 161, Cases 4 and 10, APHM.
41. Ibid.
42. Ibid., Legajo 163, Cases 1, 5, 11–12, 14; Legajo 162, Cases 1–4, 6–15, 19–15; Legajo 161, Case 3, APHM.
43. Ibid.

Chapter Five

1. Between 1952 and 1959, women distinguished themselves in all facets of the struggle against the government of Fulgencio Batista—in the different insurrectionary sectors, in the student movement, at workplaces, in the cities, and in the countryside. Among the most prominent were Gilda Parejas, who was an active student leader in the FEIM, and Leonor Arestuche and Ida Fernández, from the institute of Matanzas, who joined the youth brigade of the action and sabotage of the MR 26-7. In Cárdenas Bélica Zamora and Vivián Abreu, among many others, worked directly with the regional coordination of revolutionary activity and participated in the guerrilla movement of Las Piedras. Housewives who played an important role in various capacities included Amalia García, Irma Sánchez, Higinia García, and Juana Quintana. Veneranda Sánchez, Blanca Ojeda, and Guillermina Fernández were active in the financial sector. Verena Pino Machado became the provincial chief of clandestine operations in Las Villas. Alicia Pérez Bello was the first coordinator of MR 26-7 in Ceiba Mocha. Other coordinators included Caridad Díaz Suárez (Matanzas) and Gladys García (Cárdenas). See M. Hernández Vidaurreta, "La mujer en la revolución," *Humanismo*, 7 (January–April 1959), pp. 383–387; Gloria Marsan Sánchez, "La mujer en la lucha insurreccional cubana del 53 al 59," *OCLAE*, 6 (August 1972), pp. 7–12; Lázaro Torres Hernández, "Presencia de la mujer en la revolución cubana," *Bohemia*, 65 (June 22, 1973), pp. 100–106.
2. Interview with Ricardo González Trejo, Matanzas, 1976.
3. Frank País, "Circular interna del movimiento para los responsables," December 1956, Oficina de Asuntos Históricos, Consejo de Estado, Havana.
4. Interviews with Antonio Ñico Torres, Havana, 1989 and 1990, and Octavio Louit Venzant, Matanzas, 1989; Aldo Isidrón del Valle, "Acción revolucionaria de Guantánamo," *Revolución*, November 30, 1963, p. 5.
5. Ibid.
6. Frank País, "A los compañeros de la Dirección del 26 de Julio de toda la Isla," May 15, 1957, Oficina de Asuntos Históricos, Consejo de Estado, Havana.
7. Ibid.
8. Ibid. Frank País, "Carta de Frank País a Fidel Castro," *Revolución*, July 30, 1962, p. 13; Frank País, "La última carta de Frank a Fidel," *Revolución*, July 30, 1962, p. 10.

9. *El Imparcial,* January 5 and 18, 1957; April 26, 1957; May 17, 1957.

10. Gladys García, *Cuando las edades se pusieron de pie* (Havana, 1978). Interviews with Amador del Valle, Isidro Diez Barreras, Caridad Díaz Suárez, and Diosdado Sarmiento, Havana, 1970.

11. *El Imparcial,* May 28, 1957; March 2, 6, and 24, 1957.

12. República de Cuba, Ministerio de Defensa Nacional, Ejército, Matanzas, "Informe sobre elementos insurreccionales y actos de sabotaje," June 25, 1957; "Investigación con motivo incendio central Tinguaro," July 5, 1957, APHM.

13. E. Sosa, "Sr. O. A. Labourdette, administrator de 'La Rayonera Cubana,'" July 10, 1957, APHM.

14. *El Imparcial,* June 27 and 28, 1957, and July 3 and 22, 1957.

15. *El Imparcial,* May 30, 1957; June 10, 12, and 13, 1957.

16. Fondo Tribunal de Urgencia, Legajos 164 and 197, 1957; *El Imparcial,* June 17, 1957.

17. *El Imparcial,* July 8, 15, 22, and 26, 1957.

18. "Cienfuegos, Budapest del Caribe y primer acción de militantes pertenecientes al 26 de julio: Informa oficial del Movimiento del 26 de Julio sobre los sucesos de Cienfuegos," *Patria* (New York), December 10, 1957.

19. Fondo Tribunal de Urgencia, Legajo 171, APHM. Interviews with Amador del Valle, Leonard Arestuche, C. Garcia, and Ricardo González Trejo, Matanzas, 1976 and 1986.

20. Ibid.

21. Interview with Luis Busch, 1988 and 1989; Marcelo Fernández Font, "Plan de organización y desarrollo de la huelga general revolucionaria," 1958, History Section, Archive of the Provincial Party of Matanzas, Matanzas; "La huelga del 9 de abril de 1958," *Pensamiento Crítico,* 28 (May 1969), pp. 122–138.

22. Interviews with Isabel Zamora, Havana, 1989; Oscar Gutiérrez Barceló, Varadero, 1975; Dagoberto Díaz and Ignacio Rodríguez, Matanzas, 1982, 1987, and 1988.

23. Interviews with Alicia Pérez Bello and Arturo Lantigua, Matanzas, 1982, 1984, 1987, and 1989.

24. Interviews with Aida and Mario Manresa, Madruga, 1981; Jesús Manresa, Madruga, 1981; Israel, Dolores, Antonio, and Néstor Gil Perdomo and Juan Manuel Castillo, Matanzas, 1987 and 1988. Group reunion interview of the combatants who formed the Angel Almeijeiras Column of Havana, with the participation of Pedro Ferreiro and Carlos Manresa, Matanzas, 1988.

25. Individual interviews and group meeting with Angel Carreño Pérez, Manolo Campanioni, Roberto Pérez Serrano, Humberto Pérez, Armando Pérez Cabrera, Aníbal Amaro, Guillermo Carmenate Vizcaíno, Regio Abreu Carrillo, René Quiñones de la Osa, Carlos Martí, Gilberto Castellanos, Gabriel and Humberto Vizcaíno, Alfredo Valenzuela, Silvino Amalla, Antonio Delgado, Efraín Ojito, Liborio Cuéllar, and Carlos

Carreño, Cárdenas, 1985; Fondo Tribunal de Urgencia, Legajo 174, Case 1, APHM.

26. Interviews with Wilfredo Rodríguez and Faustino Pérez, Havana, 1988.

27. Interviews with Raúl Trujillo, Havana, 1986, 1988, and 1989; Joseíto Díaz Ramos, Pedro Betancourt, 1985, and Havana, 1986; Leonor Arestuche, Matanzas, 1981 and 1982; Andrés López Pérez, Jovellanos, 1986; Luis Fariñas, Havana, 1988; Fondo Tribunal de Urgencia, Legajo 172, Cases 12 and 14, and Legajo 175, Case 13, APHM.

28. Ibid. J. Hernández Artigas, "9 de abril de 1958: la huelga armada de Sagua la Grande," *Carteles,* 40 (February 22, 1959), pp. 38–39, 66–67; Luis Rolando Cabrera, "Sagua la Grande escribió su nombre en la historia el nueve de abril," *Bohemia,* 51 (April 5, 1959), pp. 36–39, 122–123.

29. Fondo Tribunal de Urgencia, Legajo 172, Cases 12 and 14, and Legajo 175, Case 13, APHM.

30. Fondo Tribunal de Urgencia, Legajo 174, Case 8, APHM. See also García, *Cuando las edades se pusieron de pie,* pp. 14–19.

31. Fondo Tribunal de Urgencia, Legajo 173, Case 22; José Rodríguez Castillo, "Clandestinidad en Matanzas," *Cuadernos Historicos Matanceros,* 14 (1986).

Chapter 6

1. This argument is developed by Alfred Padula, "The Fall of the Bourgeoisie, Cuba, 1959–1961" (unpublished Ph.D. dissertation, University of New Mexico, Albuquerque, 1974).

2. Interviews with Delio Gómez Ochoa, Havana, 1982, 1986; Luis Busch, Havana, 1986; Octavio Louit, Havana, 1989. The latter interview was completed with the assistance and participation of Elena Alavez. Fidel Castro, "Nombramiento del comandante Delio Gómez Ochoa como delegado de Accion," Alocución por Radio Rebelde, May 26, 1958, Sierra Maestra, Archivo de Asuntos Históricos del Consejo de Estado, Havana.

3. Interviews with Antonio López and Delio Gómez Ochoa, Havana, 1986.

4. Interviews with Jorge Serra and Olga Delgado Clavijo, Havana, 1979 and 1987; Efraín Hernández, Matanzas, 1982, 1986, and 1988.

5. Interview with Felipe Quintana, Matanzas, 1982, 1985, and 1986; "Relato sobre algunos aspectos de la lucha revolucionaria en la provincia de Matanzas a finales de 1958" (manuscript, 1983, Archivo de los Combatientes, Cárdenas).

6. Interviews with Francisco Chavarry, Havana, 1974; Felipe Quintana, Havana, 1985; Ibrahim de la Cruz, Havana, 1984. Group reunion interview with the participation of Manuel Yepe, Felipe Quintana, Verena Pino, Vivián Abreu, and Isabel Zamora, Havana, 1992.

7. Camilo Cienfuegos to Juan Ramón López Fleites, May 25, 1958, Archivos de Asuntos Históricos del Consejo de Estado, Havana. See also John Dorchester and Roberto Fabricio, *The Winds of December* (New York, 1980); Helvio Corona, "Aquellos días del sitio de Yaguajay," *Trabajo*, 4 (October 1963), pp. 30–33.

8. Interviews with Felipe Quintana, Havana, 1985 and 1985; Olga Delgado, Havana, 1979; Vicente Martínez, "La fuga de Batista," *Carteles,* 40 (January 18, 1959), pp. 4–12, 121–132, 136–138; Guillermo Villarronda, "Esto fué lo que ocurrió en Columbia después de la caída del régimen," *Bohemia*, 51 (January 11, 1959), pp. 130–136.

9. Ramón Barquín López, *Las luchas guerrilleras en Cuba: de la colonia a la Sierra* (Madrid, 1975), pp. 76–78; Roger González Guerrero, "1958: después de la gran ofensiva," *Verde Olivo*, 9 (December 22, 1968), pp. 4–9.

10. Barquín López, *Las luchas guerrilleras en Cuba*, p. 79; Florentino E. Rosell Leyva, *La Verdad* (Miami, 1960), passim; Florentino E. Rosell Leyva, "Confirma el acuerdo Batista-Cantillo," *La Crónica* (Miami), August 16, 1968, p. 19.

11. Barquín López, *Las luchas guerrilleras en Cuba,* pp. 80–81; Fidel Castro, "Revolución sí, golpe militar no," *Granma*, December 30, 1968, p. 3.

12. Fulgencio Batista, *Respuesta* (Mexico, 1960), pp. 111–112; "Cuba—Diciembre '58," *Verde Olivo*, 7 (December 31, 1966), pp. 19–29, 51; Roger González Guerrero, "Ofensiva general del Ejército Rebelde," *Verde Olivo*, 9 (December 29, 1968), pp. 4–9.

13. Batista, *Respuesta*, p. 112; Tony Fernández, "La batalla de Yaguajay," *Granma,* December 22, 1971, p. 2; William Gálvez Rodríguez, "El combate de Yaguajay," *Verde Olivo*, 9 (January 7, 1968), pp. 14–17.

14. Interviews with Manuel Yepe and Felipe Quintana, Havana, 1987; Verena Pino, Vivián Abreu, and Isabel Zamora, Havana, 1989.

15. Interview with Manuel Yepe, Havana, 1987; Gervasio G. Ruiz, "Antologia de partes oficiales: la dictadura que cayó derrotada por sus victorias," *Carteles*, 40 (January 18, 1959), pp. 26–28, 134.

16. Interview with Manuel Yepe, Havana, 1987.

Index

AAA, 40, 97
Abreu, Vivián, 123(n1)
Action groups, 63, 77, 81, 83, 84, 85, 87, 88, 90. *See also* Insurrection; Workers' cells
Acusador, El, 63
Agramonte (municipality), 6, 42, 62, 64, 94, 96, 97, 98
Agramonte, Roberto, 3
Agrícola Retiro, 67
Aguacate militia, 95
Air force, 10
Alacranes, 53, 54, 71, 79, 92
Alava sugar mill, 53, 55, 56, 57, 59, 67, 75
Alemán, Julián, 7, 16, 33, 39, 44, 45, 47; death of, 42
Alliegro, Anselmo, 103
Almeijeiras (Angel) guerrilla column, 99, 101, 102
Altos de Mompié, 100
Alturas de Madruga, 93
Alturas de Matanzas, 94
Alvarez, Onelio, 75
Alvarez de la Noval, José Miguel, 5
Alvarez Margolles, Manuel, 2
Alvarez sisal plant, 78
Amarillas, 76(table)
Amnesty, 23, 39, 67
Amparo *colonia*, 70
Angel de la Campa, Miguel, 7
Anniversary commemorations, 13, 15, 18, 19, 20, 23, 26, 68
Anticommunism, 40
April 4, 1956, rebellion, 9–10
April 9, 1958, strike, 10, 91, 93–94, 95–97, 99, 100

Aragonés, Emilio, 88
Arangueren, 78
Araujo sugar mill, 56, 67, 69
Arcos de Canasí sugar mill, 71
Arece Bank, 79
Arestuche, Leonor, 123(n1)
Argüelles, 77
Arigüanabo textile plant, 43, 45
Armed actions. *See* Guerrillas; Insurrection; Military; Rebel army; Workers' cells
Arrechabala sugar company, 16, 53, 57, 70
Arrobas, 54
Arson, 73, 76, 89, 90
Arteaga (cardinal), 52
Artemisa, 26
Association of *Colonos* (Asociación de Colonos), 36
Association of Landowners (Asociación de Hacendados), 34
Ataja, 30
Atlantic Gulf Company, 58, 59
Atrevido farm, 79, 92
Aurora distillery, 70
Australia sugar mill, 55, 56, 57, 59
Auténtico government, 1, 2, 13, 14, 38, 97; youth in, 15, 17, 28, 63. *See also* March 10, 1952, coup
Auténtico Party Organization (Organización Auténtico; OA), 7, 9, 11, 40, 105
Autobuses Modernos, 6, 72
Avila, Luis, 69
Avila (Luis) Detachment, 97, 98
Avila, Reynaldo, 82

Banaguises, 73
Bank workers, 52
Barba, Alvaro, 18, 24
Baró, Justino, 73
Barquín, Ramón, 4, 9, 106
Barrera Pérez, Pedro, 4
Base Revolutionary Cells (Celulas
  Revolucionarias de Base; CRB), 101
Batey, 54
Batista, Rubén, 20, 23, 28, 64
Batista y Zaldívar, Fulgencio, 1, 4, 40;
  first term of, 4, 7–8, 12, 61; military
  opposition to, 8–11, 82–83; 1952 coup
  by, 1–3, 4–5, 111; resignation of, 103;
  and strikes, 50, 51, 52; in sugar
  disputes, 37
Bayamo garrison attack, 21, 66, 104
Beaulac, William, 8
Becerra sisal plant, 78
Becquer, Conrado, 37, 53
Bejucal, 101
Betroma shoe distribution company, 77
Betroma textile plant, 46, 49
Bisbé, Manuel, 18
Blanco, Lázaro, 10, 98
Blanco Rico, Antonio, 29
Bohemia magazine, 25, 27
Bolondrón, 54, 92, 94, 102
Bombings. *See* Sabotage
Borbonet, Enrique, 9
Bordón, Victor, 106
Bourgeoisie, 99, 100
BRAC. *See* Bureau to Repress Communist
  Activities in Cuba
Budgets, under Batista, 35, 40–41
Bureau to Repress Communist Activities
  in Cuba (Buró de
  Repressión a las Actividades
  Comunistas; BRAC), 40
Busch, Luis, 100
Business community, 74, 81, 85, 99

Caballerías, 47
Cabañas, Tomás, 9
Cabezas, 95
Cabrera, Eugenio, 39, 42, 54, 102
Cafetal farm, 78
Calabazar textile plant, 7, 43
Calderín, Lemus, 46
Calimete, 58, 73, 76
Calixto García Hospital, 22
Calle, La (Havana), 39, 68
Camacho, Julio, 91

Camagüey, 2, 26, 27, 36, 85, 90, 104
Camaño, Eliseo, 93
Camarioca, 7, 42, 43, 46, 49, 95, 97
Camero, Manuel, 104
Canimar sugar mill, 57
Cantel, 97
Canteras, 52
Cantillo Porras, Carlos, 2, 8, 103, 104,
  106
Cantillo Porras, Eulogio, 2, 103, 104, 106
Capote, Armando, 88
Carbonera plantation, 43
Carboneras, 7
Carbó Serviá, Juan Pedro, 24, 26
Cárdenas, 10, 62, 64, 72, 81, 96, 97, 98,
  102, 123(n1); labor disputes in, 42, 45,
  49, 50, 53, 69, 71, 77; sabotage in, 47,
  52, 73, 75, 76, 78, 89, 90, 92, 94, 95;
  students in, 6, 19, 27, 79
Cárdenas Institute, 22
Cargo transportation workers, 71–72
Carlos Rojas, 53, 76(table), 78, 79, 89, 92
Carolina sugar mill, 67, 69, 71
Carratalá, Conrado, 39
Carrera Justiz, Pablo, 8
Carretera de Dubroy, 78
Carrillo, Justo, 3, 9
Carteles, 27
Casanova Orihuela, Domingo, 34, 54
Castellanos, Juan Manuel, 45
Castillo de la Punta fortress, 5
Castillo de Príncipe prison, 71
Castro, Fidel, 15, 18, 31; and declaration
  of insurgency, 39; and Echeverría, 23,
  24, 28, 29; "History Will Absolve Me"
  (speech) of, 66; and July 26 uprising,
  21, 112; in Mexico, 24, 77; MR 26-7
  leadership of, 9, 10, 63, 66, 67–68, 99,
  100; and Muñoz, 62, 64; and 1952
  coup, 18, 31; and 1958 military junta,
  103–104; and Nuiry, 30; in
  revolutionary government, 104–105,
  106–107; and Santamaría, 15, 21; and
  strikes, 70, 93
Castro, Raúl, 24, 92
Castro Porta, Germán, 70
Cayo Hueso neighborhood, 16
Cayo Loco Naval Base, 91
Ceiba Mocha, 79, 123(n1)
Ceiba Mocha guerrilla group, 94, 95
Centennial generation, 15, 31
Central Utilities Council, 35
Cepeda, Raúl, 82
Cervantes, Manuel, 26

Céspedes, Carlos Manuel de, 1
Céspedes, Miguel Angel, 7
Chavarry, Francisco, 101, 104, 106
Chemical workers, 48, 51
Chibás, Eduardo, 1, 3, 15, 25, 31, 62, 63,
  68; "The Last Knock" (speech), 65
Chibás, Raúl, 25, 100
Chiva Muerta guerrilla group, 94, 102
Chomón, Faure, 29
Cidra, 78, 95, 105
Ciego de Avila, 26
Cienfuegos, Camilo, 103, 104, 105, 106,
  107
Cienfuegos, uprising in, 10, 88, 91–92
Cigar workers, 38, 50
Cinco Hermanos farm, 78
Ciro Redondo Column, 104
Civic Resistance Movement (Movimiento
  Resistencia Cívica; MRC), 81, 85–86,
  95, 99, 100, 101
Civilian rule, 3, 8, 15, 17
Civil servants, 34, 36, 41, 51
Clinic workers, 52
Coliseo, 42, 67, 70, 76, 90, 95, 98
Colón, 62, 64, 72, 81, 97, 98, 102; labor
  disputes in, 34, 36, 38, 39, 42, 53, 55,
  59, 69; sabotage in, 52, 54, 67, 70, 75,
  76(table), 89, 90, 92, 94, 95; students
  in, 6, 19
Colonos. See Sugar farmers
Columbia colonia, 92
Columbia, Camp, 5, 7, 9, 106
Communications, Ministry of, 51, 78, 89,
  90
Communications industry: workers'
  strikes of, 51, 69; sabotage of, 39, 51,
  52, 55, 76, 83, 86, 88, 89, 90, 94, 95,
  96
Compañía Operadora Canimar, 35
Confederation of Cuban Workers
  (Confederación de Trabajadores
  Cubanos; CTC), 7, 17, 34–35, 37, 38,
  50, 52, 58, 75; and FON, 41; provincial
  and local, 38, 48, 49, 52, 69, 75; and
  worker's cells, 39
Confederation of Owners of Cuba
  (Confederación Patronal de Cuba), 33
Constitution (1940), 1, 2, 12, 17, 18, 19, 28
Consultative council, under Batista, 8
Cordage workers, 47, 78
Corona, Eduardo, 68
Corralillo, 94, 96, 98
Corral Nuevo, 69, 92
Corzo Izaguirre, Raúl, 5

Cotera, Joaquín, 44, 52
Cotorro, 45
Council of Ministers, of revolutionary
  government, 107
Coups: 1933, 1, 2, 61; 1952, 1–7, 10,
  17–20, 111; 1958 proposed, 104
CRB. See Base Revolutionary Cells
Crespo, "El Guajiro," 70
Crespo, Luis, 69
CTC. See Confederation of Cuban
  Workers
Cuba, Mario, 74
Cubana Cordage, 43
Cubana de Gomas, 69
Cubana Rayonera, 78
Cuban Consolidated Railroad, 36
Cuban Cordage, 7
Cuban Electric Company, 7, 35, 37, 51,
  76, 77, 78, 89, 90
Cuban Land Tobacco Company, 38
Cuban People's Party (Orthodox) (Partido
  del Pueblo Cubano [Ortodoxo];
  PPC[O]), 1, 2, 3, 7, 9, 11, 12, 13, 15, 17,
  20, 42, 45; and MR 26-7, 38, 63, 68,
  69, 71; in 1952 coup, 62–63, 64; youth
  of, 18, 69
Cuban Railroad Company, 38
Cuban Sugar Stabilization Institute
  (Instituto Cubano de Estabilización del
  Azucár; ICEA), 37
Cuba sugar mill, 54
Cuervo, Pelayo, 10, 18, 33
Cué Somarriba, Enrique, 9

Dámaso López estate, 92
Daniel (commander), 93, 100
Daría, Humberto, 79
Daría, Rubén, 79
Darío, Rubén, 14
Decree 805, 37
Decree 848, 44
Decree 2144, 33, 43
De la Aguilera, José María, 52
De la Campa, Miguel, 8
De la Cruz, Ibrahim, 102
De la Fe, Ernesto, 8
De Las Casas, Rodolfo, 88
De la Toriente, Cosme, 26
De la Torre, Oscar, 7
Del Casal, Julián, 14
Del Cueto, Manuel, 15, 16, 69, 90
Del Mazo, Gabriel, 14
Del Valle, Amador, 88
Del Valle (colonel), 92

Demonstrations, 6–7, 12, 16, 18, 19, 25–
26, 31, 38, 65, 68–69; student, 3, 19,
20, 26, 30. *See also* Mobilizations;
Rallies
De Nicolás, Martín, 43
Deseada sugar farms, 54
DEU. *See* Directorate of University
Students
Díaz, Dagoberto, 94
Díaz, Elio, 75
Díaz Crespo, Edilio, 39, 53, 98
Díaz Suárez, Caridad, 82, 88, 123(n1)
Díaz Tamayo (general), 10
Directorate of University Students
(Directorio Estudiantil Universitario;
DEU), 3, 31, 62
Dolores sugar mill, 42, 57
Domínguez, Clemente, 78
Domínguez, Reynaldo, 34, 54
Dos Rosas sugar mill, 58, 92
Douglas, Robert W., 41
DR. *See* Revolutionary Directorate
Driggs (colonel), 9
Dubois, Julis, 29

Echemendía Leyva, Armando, 4
Echeverría, Alfredo, 26, 27
Echeverría, José Antonio, 15, 18, 19, 20,
23, 24, 25, 26, 27, 53; death of, 30; and
DR, 28; and Fidel Castro, 23, 24, 28,
29
Eisenhower, Dwight D., 12
El Bolo sabotage group, 76, 77, 79, 94
El Cocal sabotage group, 76, 77, 79, 94
El Conde farm, 79
Electrical workers, 39, 51–52
Elena sugar mill, 58
El Morrillo, 3
El Phinney, 95, 96
El Tejar *colonia*, 70
Entidad Agapito Laurrari, 69
Entralgo, Elías, 20
Escalona Dermidio, 101
Escambray, 102
Escambray Front, 97
España Republicana sugar mill, 59
España sugar mill, 34
Espiñera, Gilberto, 93
Expeditionary landing (1956), 42, 66, 68,
72, 82; insurrection concurrent with,
74–76, 77, 78–80, 84
Esteban Garay, Angel, 65
Explosions. *See* Sabotage
Exports, sugar, 35–36

Express Services Amaro, 71

Fábrica de Hilazas Sintéticas of San José
farm, 69
Falcón Amaro, Manuel, 79
Falcón Amaro, Nicolás, 79
Falla Bonet, Fidel, 79
Farías, Gilberto, 78
Febles, Roberto, 78
Federation of Textile Workers of
Matanzas (Federación de Trabajadores
Textiles de Matanzas), 33. *See also*
National Federation of Textile Workers
FEIC. *See* Student Federation of the
Cárdenas Institute
Feijóo, Samuel, 33
FEIM. *See* Student Federation of the
Institute of Matanzas
FEN. *See* National Students' Front
Fernández, Cecilio, 79
Fernández, Guillermina, 123(n1)
Fernández, Ida, 123(n1)
Fernández, Ignacio, 94
Fernández, Mario, 22
Fernández Alvarez, Jose, 9
Fernández Font, Marcelo, 100, 107
Fernández Miranda, Roberto, 103
Ferrá, Alejandro, 16
Ferrá, Antonio, 16
Ferrá, Armelio, 16
Ferrer, Sergio, 72
Ferrocarriles Occidentales de Cuba,
73
FEU. *See* University Student Federation
Fiallo, Amalio, 25
FNTA. *See* National Federation of Sugar
Workers
FNTT. *See* National Federation of Textile
Workers
Focos, 93
Fomentos Químicos, 48
FOMN. *See* National Maritime Workers'
Federation
FON. *See* National Workers' Front
FONU. *See* National United Workers
Front
FPTT. *See* Provincial Federation of Textile
Workers
Fraga Moreno, René, 52, 64
Fraga Moreno (René) detachment, 52, 98
Francis, Osmel, 27
Franqui, Carlos, 49, 100–101
Freire, Aroldo, 79
Fumigation, 50

Gálvez, William, 106
Garcerán del Vals, José, 103
García, Amalia, 123(n1)
García, Emérito, 96
García, Gladys, 88, 123(n1)
García, Higinia, 123(n1)
García, Hugo, 78, 79
García, Pilar, 47, 51, 52, 59, 77, 89, 92, 103
García Bárcenas, Rafael, 3, 8, 9, 111
García Lorenzo, Pablo, 79
García Montes, Oscar, 8
García Morales, Hugo, 78
García Tuñón, Jorge, 4
Gil Perdomo, Israel, 95
Gil Perdomo brothers, 39, 76, 78
Gil Placencia, Agapito, 48
Goicuría Garrison, 21, 51
Gómez, Franklin, 75
Gómez García, Raúl, 64, 65
Gómez Lubián, Chiqui, 88
Gómez Ochoa, Delio, 100, 101
Gómez Sicre, Clemente, 9
González, Laudelino, 15, 16, 75
González Trejo, Ricardo, 68, 69, 75, 78, 79, 81, 82, 89, 93
Granma expeditionary forces. *See* Expeditionary landing
Grau San Martín, Ramón, 25, 62
Gravi sisal plants, 46, 74
Gualberto Gómez, Juan, 23
Guamacaro, 35, 53, 98
Guanabacoa, 45, 80
Guanajay, 7
Guantánamo, 27, 30, 84
Guantánamo Naval Base, 74
Guásimas, 97
Guedes, Leonel, 73
Guerrillas, 10, 11, 24, 93–95, 96, 97, 98, 99, 101, 102–103, 123(n1); burned, 94, 97. *See also* Rebel army
Guevara, Ernesto Ché, 100, 104
Guines, 92
Guipúzcoa Company, 92
Güira de Macurijes, 96
Guiteras, Antonio, 4, 12, 19, 23, 25, 31, 61
Gulf Atlantic, 67
Gutiérrez, Gustavo, 44
Gutiérrez, Oscar, 94
Gutiérrez Barceló, Oscar, 106

Hart Dávalos, Armando, 20, 68
Hart Dávalos, Enrique, 52, 75, 93, 94
Hart (Enrique) guerrilla groups, 97, 98,

101, 103
Havana, 2, 7, 17, 26, 27, 90, 94, 104
Haya de la Torre, Victor Raúl, 14
Hedges, Burke, 43, 75
Hemp workers. *See* Sisal workers
Henequenera Laurrari, 69
Hermida, Ramón O., 7, 34
Hernández, Ciro, 73
Hernández, Esteban, 102
Hernández, Marcos, 46, 47
Hernández, Melba, 65
Hernández, Rolando, 79
Hires Sugar Company, 92
Hirigoyen, Marcos, 6, 16
Holguín, 26, 104
Huao, Armando, 70, 81, 82, 92; death of, 93

ICEA. *See* Cuban Sugar Stabilization Institute
Imparcial, El, 22–23
Industrialists, 85
Ingenieros, José, 14
Instituto del Henequén, 7
Insurgency. *See* Insurrection
Insurrection, 13, 24, 25, 28–29, 31, 38, 39, 42, 59; expeditionary landing concurrent with, 74–76, 77, 78–80, 84. *See also* Action groups; July 26 Revolutionary Movement; Workers' movement
Intellectual class, 85
Interamerican Company, 71
Inter-American Conference (1933), 61
Inter-American Press Association, Congress of, 29, 30
Inter-American Regional Organization of Workers (Organización Regional Interamericana de Trabajadores; ORIT), 37
Interior, Ministry of, 34, 48
International Harvester Company, 45
International Sugar Agreement, 35
Irisarri, José Miguel, 3
Isabel neighborhood, 78
Itabo, 97

Jacomino, Alfredo, 7
Jagüey, 23, 56, 64, 70, 94
Jagüey Grande, 42, 55, 59, 78, 90
Jarcía, 7, 75. *See also* La Jarcía plant
José Martí People's University, 25
Jovellanos, 62, 64, 72, 74, 76(table), 81, 94, 96, 97, 102; labor disputes in, 37,

42, 46, 47, 53, 55; sabotage in, 73, 75, 92, 95; students in, 6, 19
Juan Gualberto Gómez telegraph network, 78
July 26 Revolutionary Movement (Movimiento Revolucionario 26 Julio; MR 26-7), 9, 10, 15, 17, 21–22, 27; beginnings of, 21, 63, 66, 68; CTC in, 38–39; and FEU, 28–29; leadership of, 12, 99, 100 (*see also* País, Frank); in Mexico, 24, 28, 29, 30, 42, 70; in 1958, 100–102, 103–104, 105; opposition within, 87; organization and strategy of, 16, 24, 25, 39, 42, 52, 58, 59, 63, 65–66, 67, 68, 69, 70, 72, 84, 86, 87–88, 100–102; and textile workers, 48, 49; and trade unions, 42, 47, 51, 52, 71; youth in, 25, 27. *See also* Expeditionary landing; Insurrection; Moncada garrison attack; Propaganda; Rebel army; Strikes; Workers' cells; Workers' movement

Korn, Alejandro, 14
Kuquine farm, 9

Labor, Ministry of, 47, 49, 54
Laboratory workers, 52
Labor disputes, 33, 34, 35, 36, 37, 38, 42, 43, 44, 46, 47, 50, 52–59, 60
Labor movement, 16, 41–42. *See also* National Workers' Front; Trade unions; Workers' movement
La Cabaña fortress, 5, 9, 22
La Conchita sisal plantations, 49, 50
La Conchita sugar mill, 53, 54, 71, 73
La Cordelera, 69, 97
La Cubana transport enterprise, 71
La Estrella sisal company, 45, 49
La Fermina farm, 75
La Fermina guerrilla group, 94
La Fé sisal farm, 75
Lago, Raúl, 97
La Jarcía plant, 42, 43, 44, 45, 49; workers of, 47, 48
Lantigua, Arturo, 79, 95
La Paciencia guerrilla groups, 94, 102
La Paz, 95
La Punta, 19
La Rayonera, 42, 43–44, 45, 46, 47, 48, 49, 69, 75, 80, 89
La República transport enterprise, 71
La Rosa farm, 92
Larrauri Carboneras plantations, 44, 47

Las Carboneras sisal plantations, 44, 46, 47, 69
Las Cuevas, 95
Las Mercedes, 10. *See also* Mercedes sugar mill
Las Piedras guerrilla group, 94, 102, 123(n1)
Las Villas, 2, 35, 59, 76, 88, 90, 94, 97, 100, 102, 104, 123(n1)
La Vega sugar farm, 58, 78, 92
La Vizcaya distillery, 70
Layoffs, 33, 34, 35, 36, 38, 45, 47, 48, 49–50, 55, 58, 72
Legislature, 8, 26
Léon, 92
Leonard Castell, Ignacio, 4
Liberation Action (Acción Libertadora), 9
Licorera de Cárdenas, 70
Lima, Pepe, 105
Limonar, 36, 53, 56, 69, 76
Limones sugar mill, 35, 36, 54, 55, 56, 57, 58, 59
Lineras, Pascasio, 7, 16, 42, 43, 46
Loma de Camarones, 95
Loma Phinney, 94, 96
López, Antonio, 24
López, Jaime, 42, 57, 68
López, Ñico, 68
López Blanco, Marino, 7
López Fleites, Juan Ramón, 97, 103, 106
Los Arabos, 38, 52, 54, 55, 89, 90, 94
Los Freyre, 96
Louit, Octavio, 84, 85

Maceo Column, 103, 104
Maceo Regiment, 82
Machado, Gerardo, 16
Machado, Margot, 88
Madruga, 94, 95, 101, 102, 103
Mañach, Jorge, 14
Managüa military base, 9
Mandigutía, José A., 7
Manguito, 55, 58, 67, 70, 76(table), 78
Manzanillo, 26
March 10, 1952, coup, 1–7, 10; student protest of, 17–20
March 13 Directorate. *See* Revolutionary Directorate
María Luisa farm, 78
Mariátegui, Carlos, 14
Marinello, Juan, 25
Maritime workers, 50
Mármol Díaz, José, 35

Martí (municipality), 10, 89
Martí, José, 14, 15, 21, 27, 31, 94, 96, 97
Martí (José) Column One, 100
Martín Elena, Eduardo, 2, 5, 6, 9
Martínez, Luis, 79
Martínez Planos, Gastón, 46
Massip, Salvador, 3
Matanzas, xiv(map), 2, 5, 21, 59, 70, 93, 101, 102, 123(n1); labor disputes in, 36, 43, 44, 50, 69; sabotage in, 52, 73, 74, 76, 78, 79, 80, 87, 89, 94, 95; students in, 3-4, 6-7, 17, 18, 19, 26, 30
Matanzas Institute, 18
Matanzas military garrison, 2
Matanzas Province, 11-12, 15, 103
Matanzas regiment, 9, 96, 103
Matanzas teachers' training school, 64
Máximo Gómez, 64, 76(table), 89, 97
May 8, 1952, mobilizations, 18-19
Mayor, Wilfredo, 79
McCarthy, Francis, 8
Mella, Julio Antonio, 14, 20, 25, 31
Mercedes sugar mill, 53, 55, 58, 67
Mexico letter, 28, 29
Middle classes, 41, 49, 85, 100
Miguel de los Baños, 95
Military, 1, 2, 3, 4, 5, 8; in 1957-1958, 91-92, 103-106; opposition within, 1, 2, 8-11; puros and tanquistas in, 3, 4, 5, 8, 9, 10
Military coups. See Coups
Military Intelligence Service (Servicio de Inteligencia Militar; SIM), 9, 29, 30, 72
Military juntas: 1952, 4, 7; 1959, 92, 103, 104, 106
Miranda, Fernández, 4
Miret, Pedro, 68
MNR. See National Revolutionary Movement
Mobilizations, 18-19, 27, 30, 54, 55, 66, 90. See also Demonstrations; Rallies
Mocha, 95
Moncada garrison attack, 21, 22, 23, 25, 63, 64-65, 66; amnesty for participants in, 23, 67
Moncada Project, 15, 16, 63
Monteagudo Fleites, Elías, 9
Montecristi Group, 9
Montejo, Puchín, 69
Morales, Guillermo, 10-11
Morales del Castillo, Andrés Domingo, 37
MRC. See Civic Resistance Movement

MR 26-7. See July 26 Revolutionary Movement
Mujal Eusebio, 16, 26, 38, 41, 44
Muñiz, Rolando, 78, 80
Muñoz Monroy, Mario, 15, 16, 19, 21, 61-65, 106
Muñoz (Mario) Detachment, 52, 97, 98
Murga Sibu neighborhood, 56

Naranjo colonia, 70
National Bank, 3, 40
National Federation of Sugar Workers (Federación Nacional de Trabajadores Azucareros; FNTA), 12, 17, 27, 42, 53, 54, 55, 56, 57, 58, 59
National Federation of Textile Workers (Federación Nacional de Trabajadores Textiles; FNTT), 7, 43, 44, 48
National Finance Corporation (Financiera Nacional) 37
National Harmony Commission, 11
Nationalist sentiment, 1, 2, 37-38, 40, 62. See also Patriotism
National Maritime Workers' Federation (Federación Obrera Marítima Nacional; FOMN), 50
National Revolutionary Movement (Movimiento Nacionalista Revolucionario; MNR), 8, 9, 21
National Students' Front (Frente Estudiantil Nacional; FEN), 81, 82, 99, 100
National United Workers Front (Frenta Obrero Nacional Unido; FONU), 100
National Workers' Front (Frente Obrero Nacional; FON), 41, 42, 59, 95, 100
Navy, 5, 9, 10, 88, 91
Necessary war, 15, 30
Negret, Julián, 5
New York World Telegram, 40
Nicaro nickel plant, 41
Nicolás, Digno, 55
Nuiry, Juan, 29, 30-31

OA. See Autentico Party Organization
OAS. See Organization of American States
Ojeda, Blanca, 123(n1)
Omnibus Aliados, 6
Onanay, 105
Organization of American States (OAS), 18
Oriente Province, 2, 12, 24, 25, 85, 90, 104

Orihuela Torras, José, 9
ORIT. *See* Inter-American Regional
  Organization of Workers
Orlando Rodríguez, Luis, 39
Ortodoxo Party. *See* Cuban People's Party
  (Orthodox)

País, Frank, 72, 74; death of, 90; MR 26-7
  leadership of, 81, 82–83, 85–87
País (Frank) Second Front, 100
Palmillas, 76(table)
Paneque, Diego, 101
Pardo Llada, José, 25
Parejas, Gilda, 123(n1)
Patriotism, 3–4, 13, 25, 62. *See also*
  Nationalist sentiment
Pazos, Felipe, 3
Pedraza (colonel), 39, 59
Pedro Betancourt, 53, 54, 64, 70, 78, 79,
  94, 102
Pérez, Faustino, 20, 81, 100
Pérez Bello, Alicia, 95, 123(n1)
Pérez Coujil (army officer), 53
Pérez Díaz, Artemio, 4
Pérez Falcón, Ismael, 68
Pérez Hernández, Benito, 70
Pérez Hernández, Nicolás, 8
Pérez Leyva, Angel, 78
Perico, 52, 59, 73, 76, 89, 90
Perret Foundry, 55
Peña, Erelio, 95
Pica-postas, 76, 78, 88, 94, 95
Piedra Negueruela, Orlando, 79
Pina, Verena, 105
Pinar del Río, 9, 85, 90, 97, 101, 102, 103
Piñeiro, Manuel, 69
Pino Machado, Julio, 88
Pino Machado, Verena, 102, 123(n1)
Plácido Regiment, 5, 47, 70, 74, 89
Plantanal neighborhood, 78
Platt amendment, 61
Poetry, 14
Police forces, 5, 9, 10, 22, 23, 24, 64, 78,
  79–80, 84
Pomar, Facundo, 6
Pomares, Víctor, 58
Ponte, Héctor, 69
Popular movement, 11–12, 16–17, 18,
  21
Popular Socialist Party (Partido Socialista
  Popular; PSP), 40, 52, 97, 98, 105
Por Fuerza sugar mill, 53, 56, 57
Portell Vilá, Herminio, 3
Portocarrero, Jesús A., 8

Port workers, 50, 70, 95
PPC(O). *See* Cuban People's Party
  (Orthodox)
Presidential palace, 1957 attack on, 30, 86
Prío Socarrás, Carlos, 1, 2, 3, 5, 6, 24, 25,
  31, 39
Professional classes, 6, 8, 14, 20, 21, 81,
  85, 99
Progreso sugar mill, 71, 72, 90, 92
Propaganda, 65, 66, 72–73, 74, 77, 83, 85,
  88
Provincial Federation of Textile Workers
  (Federación Provincial de Trabajadores
  Textileras; FPTT), 7, 12, 16, 44, 45, 47,
  48, 69, 75
PSP. *See* Popular Socialist Party
Public servants, 34, 36, 41
Pueblo Nuevo, 89
Puerto sugar mill, 36, 54, 58
Punta Hicacos, 103

Quemados, 94, 97
Quiala, José, 88
Química-Comercial, 48
Quintana, Felipe, 102, 103, 106
Quintana, Juana, 123(n1)

Radio stations, 30, 78, 101, 102, 106
Rafael Trejo People's University, 23
Railways: workers at, 36, 38; sabotage of,
  55, 73–74, 75, 77–78, 89, 90, 96
Rallies, 19, 20, 51, 58, 64. *See also*
  Demonstrations; Mobilizations
Ramos Latour, René, 91
Rayonera Cubana, 95
Rayon mill workers, 7, 12, 19, 43, 44, 45,
  46, 48, 75. *See also* La Rayonera
Rebel army, 10, 11, 12, 31, 39, 52, 66, 84,
  86, 93, 97, 99, 101, 102–104. *See also*
  Guerrillas
Refinery workers, 53
Rego Rubido, José, 104
Religious community, 11, 79, 99, 105
Renovation movement, 14, 15
Repression, 18, 19, 21, 22, 23, 24, 46, 47,
  64, 92, 97
Revolución, 49
Revolutionary Directorate (Directorio
  Revolucionario; DR), 12, 15, 17, 24, 28,
  29, 30, 40, 97, 105; Manifesto to the
  People of Cuba, 28
Revolutionary movement, organization
  of, 20–21. *See* Insurrection; July 26
  Revolutionary Movement; Rebel army;

Revolutionary Directorate
Rey, Fernando, 92
Rey, Santiago, 25, 26
Reyes Cairo, Julio, 16, 65
Rivero Agüero, Andrés, 8
Rivero Mechoso, Juan, 22
Robaina Piedra, Luis, 4, 103
Roca, Deodoro, 14
Rodríguez, Antonio, 73
Rodríguez, Conrado, 27, 53
Rodríguez, Francisco, 24
Rodríguez, Fructuoso, 19, 25, 26, 27, 29, 53
Rodríguez, Horacio, 42, 70
Rodríguez, Luis Orlando, 18
Rodríguez, Osvaldo, 88
Rodríguez Avilas, Pedro, 5, 103
Rodríguez Calderón, José, 5, 103
Rodríguez Llompart, Hector, 106
Roig de Leuchsenring, Emilio, 14
Rojas González, Juan, 4, 103
Roman Catholic Church, 11
Roosevelt, Elliot, 8
Roque, 90
Rosell Leyva, Florentino, 104
Rubén Batista Literacy Campaign, 23
Rubio, Martín, 67
Rural guard, 54, 58, 74, 89
Río Chaviano (general), 104

Sabotage, 31, 65, 70, 77–78, 80, 83, 85–86, 87, 88, 90, 92, 112. *See also* Electrical workers; Sugarcane field burnings; *under* Communications industry; Railways; Sisal workers; Utilities
Sáez, Enrique, 97
Sagua la Grande, 96
Saladrigas, Carlos, 8
Saladrigas Zayas, Enrique, 8
Salas Cañizares, Rafael, 4, 5, 26, 37, 105; death of, 30
Salvador, David, 100
San Antonio de Cabezas, 79
Sánchez, Calixto, 16
Sánchez, Irma, 123(n1)
Sánchez, Universo, 68, 69
Sánchez, Veneranda, 82, 123(n1)
Sánchez Arango, Aureliano, 6
Sánchez Cervantes, Alejandro, 94
San Claudio de Coliseo farm, 92
Sandarán, Rolando, 75
San Fabián, 95
San Ignacio sugar mill, 96

San José de las Lajas, 45
San José de los Ramos, 55, 94
San Juan, 95
San Julián sugar farm, 67
San Miguel, 98
San Miguel de los Baños, 105
San Nicolás distillery, 70
San Pedro Apóstol parish, 80
San Rafael farm, 78
San Román, Manuel, 91
Santa Ana-Cidra, 102
Santa Catalina estate, 90
Santa Clara, 26, 27, 30, 85, 88, 104
Santa Lucía sugar farm, 67
Santamaría, Aldo, 48, 68, 69, 72, 74–75, 78, 79
Santamaría, Abel, 15, 21, 63, 64
Santamaría, Haydée, 65, 100
Santa Rita sugar mill, 56
Santiago de Cuba, 21, 25, 26, 27, 30, 38, 79, 82, 84, 90, 93, 104
Santiago de Las Vegas, 38
Santiesteban, José, 79
Santo Domingo sugar mill, 55, 71
SAR. *See* Society of Friends of the Republic
Sarmiento, Diosdado, 88
Saturnino Lora Hospital, 64
September 4, 1933, coup, 1, 2
Septembristas, 2, 4, 5, 8, 10
Sergeants' Revolt, 1
Shoe workers, 51
Sierra de Bibanasí, 94, 96, 102
Sierra de los Organos, 101
Sierra Maestra, 10, 11, 30, 63, 78, 86, 99, 100–101
SIM. *See* Military Intelligence Service
SIR, 70, 77
Sisal workers, 42, 44, 47, 48, 49, 50; and sabotage, 75, 76, 78, 95; strikes of, 7, 16, 33, 43, 45, 46, 69
Smith Comas, José, 15, 70
Socialist Party, 12
Social movements, origins of, 13–15, 62
Society of Friends of the Republic (Sociedad de Amigos de la República; SAR), 25, 27
Sogo, Dámaso, 4, 5
Soledad sugar mill, 37, 55, 73
Soler, Eugenio, 6
State security forces, 18
Street actions. *See* Demonstrations
Strikes, 2, 6, 50, 51, 52, 106; April 1958, 10, 91, 93–94, 95–97, 99, 100; and

FEU, 28, 29; and Granma landing, 84; in insurrection strategy, 16, 17, 24, 28, 29, 30, 31, 38, 63, 69, 70, 72, 106; and MRC, 85–86; student-worker, 6, 17–18, 25, 30; training for, 84. *See also* Work stoppages; *under* Communications industry; Sisal workers; Sugar workers; Textile workers
Student Directorate (1930), 20
Student Federation of the Cárdenas Institute (Federación Estudiantil del Instituto de Cárdenas; FEIC), 15, 19
Student Federation of the Institute of Matanzas (Federación Estudiantil del Instituto de Matanzas; FEIM), 6, 11, 12, 15, 17, 18, 19, 20, 21, 22, 26, 123(n1)
Student movement, 3, 9, 21, 23, 24, 26, 29, 31, 100; demonstrations of, 3, 26, 30; as generational movement, 6, 13–15, 21, 29; government repression of, 21–22, 23, 25, 26; and 1952 coup, 6–7, 17–20, 111; and worker solidarity, 3, 12, 17, 27, 41. *See also* National Students' Front; Student Federation of the Cárdenas Institute; Student Federation of the Institute of Matanzas; University Student Federation
Suero, Fernández, 89
Sugarcane field burnings, 31, 34, 53, 54, 56, 57, 65, 67, 70, 73, 75, 76(table), 83, 92, 120(n54)
Sugar exports, 35–36
Sugar farmers, 33, 34, 36, 37, 54, 59
Sugar mills, 34, 36, 37, 42, 53, 54, 55, 56, 57, 58, 59, 67, 70, 71, 73, 90, 92, 96. *See also* Alava sugar mill; Limones sugar mill; Tinguaro sugar mill; Zorrilla sugar mill
Sugar workers, 89, 96, 99–100; labor disputes of, 33, 34, 35, 36, 37, 42, 52–59; strikes, 12, 17, 27, 53, 55, 57, 58, 67, 69–71, 77, 83. *See also* National Federation of Sugar Workers; Sugarcane field burnings
Susana sugar farms, 54

Tabernilla Dolz, Francisco, 2, 4, 5, 10, 37
Tabernilla Palmero, Francisco, 103
Tánes, Israel, 69
Tank officers. *See under* Military
Tápanes, Israel, 16, 82
Telegraph. *See* Communications industry
Telephone. *See* Communications industry

Textile imports, 33, 43
Textilera Ariguanabo, 7
Textile workers, 3, 7, 16, 33, 38, 42, 43, 44, 47–48; strikes of, 7, 33, 43–44, 45, 46, 49. *See also* National Federation of Textile Workers; Rayon mill workers
Tinguaros, 57
Tinguaro sugar mill, 34, 54, 57, 58, 59, 67, 77, 89
Tire workers, 51
Tobacco Stabilization Fund, 3
Torres, Antonio, 100
Torres, Joaquín, 42, 49, 78, 81, 82, 93
Torres, Juan Manuel, 68
Torres, Ñico, 84
Torres, Pedro, 48
Trade unions, 7, 16, 50, 51, 52, 57; and MR 26-7, 42, 47, 51, 52, 71; and repression, 41, 48, 75; strike training for, 84; student actions for, 6, 12; and sugar workers, 53, 54, 55, 57, 58, 59; textile workers, 7, 16, 44, 45, 47–48. *See also* Confederation of Cuban Workers
Tráfico y Transporte, 71
Transportation workers, 38, 50, 51, 71, 72; and disruptions, 94, 95, 96
Trejo, Rafael, 25
Triunfo sugar mill, 92
Trujillistas, 10
Trujillo, Raúl, 96
Truslow Mission Plan, 13, 35

Underground, 21, 39, 77, 89, 91, 92, 93, 97, 99, 101, 102
Unión de Reyes, 21, 42, 53, 55, 71, 72, 73, 79, 81, 92
United Nations, 18
United States, 3, 8, 11, 12, 24, 37, 38, 40, 41, 91; revolutionary activity in, 68, 100
University of Havana, 6, 8, 18, 20, 22, 24, 26, 28, 30, 39
"University of the Airwaves" (television program), 20
University reform, 14, 25
University Student Federation (Federación Estudiantil Universitaria; FEU), 2, 6, 11, 12, 15, 17, 18, 19, 20, 23, 24, 25, 26, 27, 30, 31, 39; Declaration of Principles, 7; and Moncada amnesty, 67; and MR 26-7 28–29, 64; and sugar workers, 53, 57
Uría, Pedro, 6
U.S. Steel Company, 8

Utilities, 35; sabotage of, 35, 76, 78, 83, 88, 94, 95. *See also* Communications industry

Valdés Daussá, Ramiro, 25
Valle de Guamacaro, 103
Varadero, 89, 97, 103
Varela Castro, Manuel, 9
Vargas Vila, 14
Vasconselos, José, 14
Vedado Institute, 25
Vega, José, 46
Vera, Eliseo, 78
Veradero, 45
Verdayes, Antonio, 76
Verdugo, Carlos, 20
Versalles, 73, 78
Vieja Bermeja neighborbood, 79
Villa Clara Regiment, 91
Villafaña, Manuel, 9
Villamar, 77

Wage disputes, 34, 36–37, 41, 44, 47, 49, 50, 52, 53
Washington sugar mill, 70
Water supplies, 95
Weapons acquisition, 72, 74–75, 77, 80, 95, 97, 100
Western Railways, 72, 89
Women, 82, 90, 123(n1)

Workers' congress, 99
Workers' cells (sections), 12, 16, 21, 39, 41, 42, 46, 59, 63, 64, 71, 72, 81, 83, 84, 85, 86, 100. *See also* Base Revolutionary Cells
Workers' movement, 8, 14, 17, 99, 100; in MR 26-7, 38, 39–40, 42, 66; and student solidarity, 5, 12, 17, 27, 31, 41. *See also* Confederation of Cuban Workers; Workers' cells
Work slowdowns, 43, 44, 48
Work stoppages, 26–27, 43, 44–45, 51, 54, 84

Yaguajay, 103
Yaguajay garrison, 103, 104
Yaguasa sugar farm, 56
Yepe, Manuel, 101, 105
Yepe, Roberto, 106
Young Cuba (Joven Cuba), 4
Youth Brigades, 69
Youth Directorate of Matanzas, 18
Youth movement, 6, 8, 13–14, 21, 24, 25
Yumurí henequen company, 44, 48
Yumurí tire plant, 51

Zamora, Bélica, 123(n1)
Zorrilla sugar mill, 36, 38, 39, 53, 54, 56, 57, 58, 59, 67

About the Book

Based on previously untapped primary sources, this book examines the social forces that were released and shaped by the Cuban revolutionary war and, not least, the actions of real men and women attempting to forge a new future.

García's focus on Matanzas Province—an area highly representative of Cuba in demographics, racial patterns, economy, and education—allows a discussion of larger issues about the origins, character, and evolution of the armed struggle against Batista. García argues that the resistance to Batista developed in response principally to local grievances that affected a wide cross-section of the social strata; Fidel Castro's July 26 Movement was able to forge a national revolution with such vitality and appeal precisely because it addressed those local issues.

Among the archival records García drew on for the book are the testimonies and depositions of hundreds of men and women captured and tried by the Batista government. García also interviewed many of the leaders, combatants, laborers, and peasants who participated in various phases of the insurgency. The resulting study illustrates the development of methods of resistance, the evolution of varieties of rebellion, and how disparate social groupings merged into a single revolutionary movement that swept away not only an unpopular government but also an entire social system.

Gladys Marel García-Pérez is on the research staff of the Institute of History and the Center for Martí Studies, both in Havana. She was formerly with the Institute of Social Sciences at the Cuban Academy of Science. Her previous books include *Cuando las edades llegaron a estar de pie, Historia del movimiento obrero cardenense,* and (as coauthor) *Atlas historico-biografico José Martí.*